Praise for Mensch•Marks

"These unpretentious but powerful reflections provide a refreshing reprieve from the cynicism and distrust so pervasive today. No bromides or buzzwords here, this book relies on bluntly real, clear-eyed observation over a professional lifetime. They speak to the truth and force of love—the caring and compassion of a *mensch* through action not mere words. Rabbi Hammerman's wit and wisdom are no surprise to me; he is my rabbi. But the full tableau of his personal experiences and insights is extraordinary. His stories about his relationship with his brother, who is developmentally challenged, are especially moving. Each reader will find individual meaning and message that hits home. In *Mensch•Marks*, Joshua Hammerman has provided a prescription for ways to live a more human and humane life."

—US Senator Richard Blumenthal

"It's rare to find a rabbi willing to put his foibles and faith on the page with as much honesty and fervor as Rabbi Joshua Hammerman offers in this addictive volume. Each chapter is its own gem, and every story becomes a reader's personal challenge—to look at how we move through the world, especially in this divisive moment. Kudos to Rabbi Hammerman for reminding us what to strive for, and doing it with a deft pen and a great sense of humor and humility."

—**Abigail Pogrebin**, author of *My Jewish Year: 18 Holidays, One Wondering Jew*

"Using wisdom from Hillel to Winnie-the-Pooh, Rabbi Hammerman has written a book that will make this world a kinder, gentler place. I'll be recommending it to both my nice friends and the cranky ones, too."

—**A.J. Jacobs**, *New York Times* bestselling author, *The Year of Living Biblically: One Man's Humble Quest to Follow the Bible as Literally as Possible*

"In this age, when leadership and morality often seem to have nothing in common, Rabbi Joshua Hammerman offers us a window into a deeply lived life. From a genuine mensch, we learn what it is to live a life measured by moral growth and devotion to people and causes beyond us. Reading *Mensch•Marks* is bound to leave us all determined to live better lives and be better people."

—**Daniel Gordis**, author, *Israel: A Concise History of a Nation Reborn*

"For the 'hassled masses' here is an invaluable guide written with clarity, wit and humility. Whatever path you are on, Rabbi Hammerman has been there and will point to the sites and stumbling blocks."

—**Rabbi David Wolpe**, author, *David: The Divided Heart*

"Perhaps the most important characteristic of leaders—especially religious leaders—is a deep awareness of their own humanity. *Mensch•Marks,* written with verve and even chutzpah, depicts the pursuit of wisdom amidst the daily challenges and grace notes of life. Rabbi Joshua Hammerman engages readers with honesty and humor, allowing us to look more deeply at our own lives."

—**Sr. Mary C. Boys**, Vice President of Academic Affairs and Dean, Union Theological Seminary in the City of New York

"What a read! If a rabbi's job is to shake, rattle, and roll, Rabbi Hammerman is doing it. What he says is powerful and often profound, but how he says it is delightful, funny, clever, often poetic, always interesting. It's a life guide you should buy for someone who doesn't think he or she needs it. Then buy one for yourself. If everyone read *Mensch•Marks* the world would be a much kinder, saner, better place. If Rabbi Hammerman were not a father, husband, philosopher, psychologist, journalist, world traveler, life guide, humorist, humanist, traditionalist, rebel, Talmudist, mohel, and mensch, he could not have written this book. I can't wait for the movie!"

—**Alan Kalter,** renowned television announcer and the voice of *Late Night with David Letterman*

"A beautiful, warm, intimate book about the daily struggle to be a good human being."

—**Peter Beinart,** author, *The Crisis of Zionism*

"If I could recommend just one book to every rabbi and politician in America, this would be it. A master class in what it means to be a mensch from one of the nation's most gifted rabbi–writers."

—**Jonathan D. Sarna**, University Professor and Joseph H. and Belle R. Braun Professor of American Jewish History, Brandeis University

"You read Rabbi Joshua Hammerman's essays for the pure pleasure of his company, for the surprising connections he draws, for the deftness and humor with which he applies ancient teachings to 21st-century dilemmas. Rabbi Hammerman doesn't preach from on high. He speaks with the wisdom of a scholar and the generosity of a friend. You will be comforted and inspired by his example, enlightened and enriched by his words."

—**Lauren Redniss,** McArthur Foundation "Genius Grant" fellow, National Book Award finalist, Pulitzer Prize nominee, and author *of Radioactive: Marie & Pierre Curie, A Tale of Love and Fallout*

"This is an eloquent story of one rabbi's determination to learn lessons from text and from life and to share that knowledge while wrestling with faith, with loss, and with change. Rarely are people so honest, personal, and straightforward, sharing their thoughts and, even more rarely, speaking openly of their failures. Rabbi Hammerman puts values front and center. He is a mensch, and this book gives that word new meaning, making it clear that we can each develop this capacity over time."

—**Ruth Messinger**, Global Ambassador and former President and CEO, American Jewish World Service

"This is a deeply moving book... Miraculously, Hammerman has managed to maintain his decency, genuine concern for people, embrace of life—and a grounding sense of humor—through decades of an exhausting career with inexhaustible demands that empties all too many practitioners of their humanity.... One section of the book is titled "The Nobility of Normalcy." This whole book is a testament to the nobility of a normal (albeit high level) rabbinic life career and to the nobility in people living normal lives: practicing monogamy, visiting the sick, travelling outdoors through nature in wonder, suffering pain with dignity, shopping, exhibiting their Jewishness proudly, setting boundaries that protect their personal standards, balancing work and family. Hopefully, this book will inspire many to aspire to become *menschen*. At the least, reading this book will give you an unforgettable model of how to be a mensch, which many a reader will summon to inspire his or her own journey to *mentschlichkeit*."

—**Rabbi Dr. Irving "Yitz" Greenberg**, founding Director of the President's Commission on the Holocaust, Chair of the U.S. Holocaust Memorial Museum, founding President of the Jewish Life Network

Mensch• Marks

Life Lessons of a Human Rabbi
Wisdom for Untethered Times

Joshua Hammerman

Health Communications, Inc.
Deerfield Beach, Florida

www.hcibooks.com

**Library of Congress Cataloging-in-Publication Data
is available through the Library of Congress**

© 2019 Joshua Hammerman

ISBN-13: 978-07573-2177-1 (Paperback)
ISBN-10: 07573-2177-1 (Paperback)
ISBN-13: 978-07573-2178-8 (ePub)
ISBN-10: 07573-2178-X (ePub)

Publisher: Health Communications, Inc.
　　　　　3201 S.W. 15th Street
　　　　　Deerfield Beach, FL 33442–8190

Cover design by Barbara Aronica-Buck
Interior design and formatting by Lawna Patterson Oldfield
Author photo by Aviva Maller Photography

CONTENTS

PART SIX: Failure, Forgiveness, Justice, and Kindness

ACKNOWLEDGMENTS

Thishis book's publication coincides with the thirtieth anniversary of my tenure at Temple Beth El in Stamford, Connecticut. Thousands of people have come into my life over that span, and each one has made an indelible impression. I am beyond grateful to those who have learned, laughed, and cried with me and who have placed their trust in me. All of them have been cherished co-travelers on this journey and are present in this book, but I am especially appreciative of those who have taken on leadership roles. The same holds true for friends from prior pulpits in Peekskill and Beacon, New York, and elsewhere in my past, people like Rabbi Michael Schorin, Al and Betsy Bergman and Jack and Barbara Levitz. Many local rabbis, cantors, other Jewish professionals, and my clergy colleagues of other faiths have worked with me to heal the world. My interfaith partners who have assisted me most to appreciate our overwhelming similarities and occasional flashes of divergence include Kate Heichler (whose friendship at my greatest time of need can never be properly repaid), Mark Lingle, Douglas McArthur, Ann Schmidt, Dr. Kareem Adeeb, and Lisa Lynne Kirkpatrick of Grace Farms Foundation.

I'm also thankful to those who have partnered with me professionally at TBE, including some of the most talented and dedicated clergy, educators, and administrators around. My current professional partners include the incomparable Cantor Magda Fishman, Hazzan

Emeritus Sidney Rabinowitz, Lisa Gittelman-Udi, Steve Lander, Jami Fener, Mindy Rogoff, Ellen Gottfried, Linda Rezak, Beth Silver, Alberto Eyzaguirre, and Rad Vazquez, as well as the omnipresent Eileen Rosner and the latest in a string of superb temple presidents, Carl Weinberg. I am no less appreciative of the many who have worked with me in the past, some of whom remain cherished friends to this day. It was thrilling that Cantors George Mordecai and Deborah Jacobson could join us at the thirtieth anniversary concert. A special thanks to Rabbi Alex Goldman of blessed memory, who brought me to Stamford to be his assistant rabbi in 1987.

I'm especially grateful to those who spearheaded this book project in its earliest stages, including Beth Boyer, Barbara Aronica-Buck, who designed this book's cover, Gail Gruber Trell, Mindy Rogoff, Lisa Manheim, and photographer Aviva Maller, along with the book's sponsors, including the families of Ronnie and Ed Fein, Sue Frieden, Sari and Alan Jaffe, Devra Jaffe-Berkowitz and Parry Berkowitz, Betsy and Peter Kempner, Lois Stark and Gary Lessen, Norma and Milton Mann (both of blessed memory), Eileen Rosner, Beth El's Men's Club and Sisterhood, Leo P. Gallegher Funeral Home, Marsha Kaiser Shendell, Steve and Miriam Sosnick, Carl and Dana Weinberg, Dan and Sheryl Young, Sheila Romanowitz, Gary and Phyllis Gladstein and Michael Horowitz. All have encouraged and supported me in myriad ways throughout this journey.

I've had an abundance of great teachers, too many to list here, but my evolving perspective has been greatly influenced by such contemporary visionaries as Irving (Yitz) Greenberg, Joseph Telushkin, Arthur Green, Zalman Schachter Shalomi, Neil Gillman, Eugene Borowitz, David Hartman, and Jacob Neusner.

Many editors have helped nurture my writing career, none more than *The New York Jewish Week* editor and publisher Gary Rosenblatt, who first showed faith in me way back when I was in journalism school. I also am indebted to Miriam Herschlag at the *Times of Israel*, Andrew Silo-Carroll at JTA, Lauren Markow, formerly at the *Religion News Service*, and Eric Copage, former editor at *The New York Times Magazine*, for featuring my work. A special thanks to the *Religion News Association* for recently honoring me with an award for excellence in commentary in religion reporting (appropriately, I got "honorable *menschen*").

It was natural that the journey of *Mensch•Marks* to publication would be lovingly guided by HCI Books, publishers of my first book several years ago. I am grateful to the entire team and especially to Christine Belleris, who recognized the broad-based potential of this book, and Kim Weiss, who has helped me share my ideas with the world, along with Erin K. Brown, Anthony Clausi, Lawna Patterson Oldfield, Larissa Hise Henoch, and others who helped bring this book to print, plus Meryl Moss and her publicity team, with an added thank-you to Tracy Minsky.

Finally, a shout-out to my large extended and immediate family, with special thanks to my cousins Stu Zicherman and Ken Davidoff. I love them all. But I am nothing without Mara, who has been with me for the entirety of this journey, playing the dual role of life partner and best friend; and Ethan and Dan, who, like their mom, have been an unending source of strength and love. The greatest compliment I can give my sons is that they've turned out to be such *menschen*, like their mom and all four of their grandparents. Dan, Ethan, and Mara inspire me every moment of every day.

This book is dedicated to my parents, whom I discuss in the Introduction. To paraphrase the late singer-songwriter Dan Fogelberg, their blood runs through my instrument, their song is in my soul.

IMPERFECTION
An Interpretation of Psalm 99

"Adonai, You have answered them,
as the One who could bear their imperfections,
after exacting a penalty for what they did"

God could bear the imperfections of Moses, Aaron and Miriam
So why can I not forgive my own?

For You it is all so simple
Sin, punishment, repentance, slate cleaned.
The never-ending cycle
Never ends in pain.
The pain comes and goes;
The guilt is gone,
Only to return with the next golden calf.
The pain is gone, the memory is short.
It's so un-Jewish!

And so un-me!
I cannot forgive myself so easily;
For last week's indiscretions.
Missing my child's bedtime
Or missing a meeting;
Forgetting a call
Or making it.
Not hearing one cry,
Because I'm listening to another.
Or not listening hard enough to either.

You who suffers our insufferableness,
Grant me the ability to bear my own suffering.
Teach me, O paradigm of Perfection, how you stomach us,
So that I may forgive myself
For not being You.

—*Rabbi Joshua Hammerman*

INTRODUCTION
Mensch•Marks

"Man, the prisoner of nature, becomes free
by becoming fully human."

—*Erich Fromm*

In the Talmud, Hillel the sage states, "In a world that lacks human-ity, be human." If you—like most people—are concerned about the rancor that has poisoned public life, you are holding in your hand an antidote. In a world as dehumanizing as ours has become, simply being a kind, honest, and loving person, a man or woman of integrity, has become a measure of heroism—and at a time when norms of civility are being routinely quashed, it may be the only measure that matters. Hillel is saying that when everything seems to have become unhinged around you, just persevere with the singular focus of being the best human being you can be and everything else will follow from that. If you can get your own act together, at some point others will follow your lead.

It's like the story of the man outside the gates of Sodom, warning the people to stop their sinning, a legend popularized by Elie Wiesel:

He went on preaching day after day, maybe even picketing. But
no one listened. He was not discouraged. He went on preaching for
years. Finally, someone asked him, "Rabbi, why do you do that? Don't
you see it is no use?" He said, "I know it is of no use, but I must. And
I will tell you why: in the beginning I thought I had to protest and
to shout in order to change them. I have given up this hope. Now I
know I must picket and scream and shout so that they should not
change me."

And, I would add, if we cultivate civility and integrity with dogged
persistence, we will eventually change them, too.

I've devoted my life to trying to become a more fully realized, morally evolved human being, a person of character.

Jews have a word for that: *mensch.*

One isn't born a *mensch.* Nor is it a status that one ever completely
achieves; for to boast that you are *mensch* is, by definition, not to possess the requisite humility to be one. Becoming a mensch is a lifelong
process, a journey, an aspiration.

Joseph Campbell writes in *The Hero with a Thousand Faces,* "A
hero ventures forth from the world of common day into a region of
supernatural wonder—fabulous forces are there encountered, and
a decisive victory is won. The hero comes back from this mysterious
adventure with the power to bestow boons on his fellow man."

For the *mensch,* the journey to moral maturity is no less heroic,
if perhaps a little less dramatic and a lot less bloody. But unlike with
Campbell's mythic hero, in the end there is no decisive victory, because
this is a journey *with* no end. Every Bar or Bat Mitzvah video notwithstanding, one can never stop, look up at the heavens, and say, "Today I
am a *mensch.*" More accurately, the student should say, "Today, I have
started the process toward becoming a *mensch.*"

While it's unseemly to call yourself a *mensch,* for Jews there is no greater honor than for another person to call you one, indicating that, while the process of growth never ends, you've passed a threshold whereby others view you as a human of exemplary character. I often use the expression when eulogizing someone, but never have I said, "She was a billionaire," or, "He wrote a dozen bestsellers." There is something about "*mensch*" that transcends professional success. Our jobs do not define us; neither do our homes, cars, and stock portfolios. What defines us, ultimately, are our relationships, our integrity, the love we give, the love we receive.

Leo Rosten, who wrote *The Joy of Yiddish*, defines *mensch* as "someone to admire and emulate, someone of noble character." Dr. Saul Levine writes in *Psychology Today*, "The admirable traits included under the rubric of *mensch* read like a compendium of what Saints or the Dalai Lama represent to many, or others whom you might think merit that kind of respect. These personality characteristics include decency, wisdom, kindness, honesty, trustworthiness, respect, benevolence, compassion, and altruism."

But one does not need to be a saint just to be a decent, thoughtful person. To be a morally evolved human being means in fact to be fallible and imperfect, but always striving to do better. It means to seek justice but never at the expense of compassion. It means to connect, to family, to one's people, and to one's home. It means to seek transcendence, to see the extraordinary in the ordinary, to love unconditionally, to serve a higher cause, and to live a life of dignity and integrity.

Incidentally, although in German the term clearly refers to males and connotes masculinity (or, in the case of Nietzsche, *uber*-masculinity) for Jews it is not gender-specific—a woman can be a *mensch*, too. I was perusing Amazon for early Hanukkah gifts the other day and came across this mug:

Photo courtesy of Foxymug

In every respect, for her compassion, courage, and ability to forge common ground with ideological opponents, Ruth Bader Ginsburg is the quintessential wo-*mensch*.

So, let me tell you about my life path toward *mensch*-hood and how, while it may or may not have achieved the notoriety of Campbell's mythic heroes, in some ways it's been downright biblical.

According to the Book of Numbers, the Israelites made forty-two stops as they wandered from Egypt to the Promised Land. Jewish and Christian commentators alike assign this number spiritual significance, some associating those way stations with what medieval Kabbalists believed to be the forty-two letter name of God. The father of modern Hasidism, the Baal Shem Tov, said that the forty-two stations represent the stages of a person's life. Rabbi Simon Jacobson, noting that the Hebrew word for Egypt, *Mitzrayim*, also means "narrow places," writes, "All the forty-two journeys are about freeing ourselves and transcending the constraints and limitations (*Maytzarim*) of our material existence which conceals the Divine, subduing and sublimating the harsh 'wilderness' of selfish existence, and discovering the 'Promised Land'—a life of harmony between body and soul."

In the following pages, I share forty-two stepping stones along my own path of growth, with each challenge yielding significant insights that have helped me to bring God's love into the world. Bahya Ibn Pakuda, a tenth-century Jewish philosopher, wrote, "Days are like scrolls . . . write on them only what you want remembered." This book represents my personal Torah scroll, the sacred text of my life experience, incorporating lessons I have learned during my winding, tortuous journey through the Wilderness. These way stations have been the nexus where the mythological trials of Campbell's hero have met the all-too-real predicaments of a current-day rabbi, the drama played out not in the belly of a whale but in the aisles of Walmart, their sacred lessons emanating not from within a Joban Whirlwind but from the creamy interior of an Oreo cookie. The road map through my forty-two stations is best depicted not by Waze or Rand McNally, but through the *Periodic Table of Being a Mensch* that you see below.

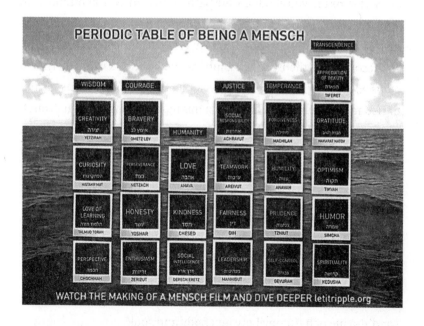

The table was created by Tiffany Shlain and Let it Ripple Film Studio (*letitripple.org*) for the ten-minute film, *The Making of a Mensch*. It incorporates Hebrew categories of character development popularized by the nineteenth-century movement known as *Mussar*, a philosophical school that is gaining renewed popularity today. These twenty-four qualities meld neatly into the forty-two stepping stones of my journey. This table is not like a game board, where the boxes may increase in value as you progress along the selected path. Rather, these character traits are of nominally equivalent value and they need to be cultivated simultaneously, for they interact and reinforce one another. A sense of justice is enhanced by accumulated wisdom and courage, and humor and humility go hand in hand. This periodic table is really an interactive 3-D network of human strivings, presented here imperfectly on a one-dimensional grid.

The brief essays in this book are organized into categories of character, benchmarks of "*menschiness*" (or, to use the Yiddish term, *menschlichkeit*). Each chapter describes a Mensch•Mark, one stepping stone toward spiritual maturation. This search for personal grounding chronicles how I've struggled to transcend pain, to overcome the errors of youth and the perils of aging, to grow from failure, to balance the parental and pastoral, to navigate the shifting tides of post-Holocaust Judaism, to cherish the sanctity of life and the holiness of the everyday, and to overcome my own innate cynicism, seeking a purer faith of affirmation, trust, kindness—and forgiveness.

These themes have been guiding principles of my life's message, each one becoming dominant at various times, and at other times receding into the background while they also interact and reinforce one another. These Mensch•Marks (okay, please indulge me if you think the term is corny), presented thematically rather than chronologically, are the points of reference through which I have constantly recalibrated my compass, and they are the life lessons through which my journey will be assessed by my children after I am gone. I hope some of these Mensch•Marks will inspire you as well.

If at the end of the day, I have helped to nurture and raise a family—and a congregation—filled with *real menschen* (the plural of *mensch*), that will be just fine with me. If by sharing what I've learned, I can bring just a bit more decency to a world that has lost its moral moorings, a modicum of generosity, honesty, and human connection in a world overflowing with cruelty, loneliness, and deceit, then I'll have made it to my personal Promised Land. I'll have done my job.

I'm an optimist. I believe that we can turn things around one *mensch* at a time.

Being a rabbi has helped me to help many others—and myself—along the path toward finding wholeness and holiness on a human level. For my very job *is* to be human—and to show others how. As I wrote in *The New York Times Magazine* back when I was twenty-eight, which is now (gasp) over three decades ago:

> *As I see it, I am a spiritual leader simply because I want to refine my own spirit, to stretch myself, using the texts of my tradition for guidance, and, in doing so, possibly to inspire others to do the same.*

I love my work because, in an age of self-driving cars, computerized Jeopardy champions, and ubiquitous robocalls, mine is one of the few professions that can never be outsourced to a machine. There is no Rabbi Robot. When it comes to nurturing human qualities, rabbis and other clergy have a distinct experience advantage that can be very beneficial in helping others to confront contemporary challenges to civility and integrity.

Look what's happened to leisure time, which many consider to be a fundamental human need. Rabbis know all about the loss of leisure time—we had to be on the job 24/7 long before the rest of America began seeing their working hours seeping into vacations and weekends. Now, just about everyone must deal with emails elbowing their way onto our beach chairs, barbecues, and soccer sidelines. How can we carve out opportunities to stop and smell the roses, experience transcendence, and take in the inherent beauty of life? Mensch•Mark 19 will help show you how.

What about privacy? "I never found the companion that was so companionable as solitude," wrote Henry David Thoreau. But over the past several years, Americans have seen a precious wall of privacy crumble before their eyes, with so much information about each of us now being shared in social media—or more surreptitiously. Rabbis saw those barriers crumble long ago. Long before Facebook, our lives were already an open book. As one who grew up in the fishbowl as a PK (preacher's kid), I know! And I can help you cope with it. See Mensch•Marks 1 and 13, for starters.

And when it comes to promoting mindfulness in daily living (something so many people are trying to do these days), or seeking kindness in an increasingly cruel landscape, or, at a time of unprecedented mobility, yearning for a sense of rootedness—well, rabbis have a two-millennium head start in dealing with all of these. A whole bunch of Mensch•Marks will help you understand that; you can start with Mensch•Marks 4, 32, and 41.

Face it, with little privacy or downtime and a whole lot of moral challenges to juggle, you are all becoming a lot like me. These days, *everyone's* becoming clergy—and we clergy have lots of lessons to share about being human in the twenty-first century.

Unlike a tell-all memoir, there are parts of my life that will not be all-told here. An important yardstick in building a *menschlicht* life is the ability to preserve a smidgen of privacy in a world where so little of it remains. My marriage, which has been incredibly stable and loving, is primarily off-limits here. I speak a lot about the challenges of parenting, but my children's adult lives are also allowed to recede respectfully into the background. My pets, however, are fair game. And the marriage between myself and my congregation, which has also been long and stable, is detailed here very selectively and (I hope) sensitively. I'm not writing this to settle scores or to feed into the lurid appetites of an insatiable zeitgeist, but rather to respond to my father's clarion call to me: *"Be a mensch."*

So, given what I've just written, I must include this disclaimer right from the start. My life has been b-o-r-i-n-g, at least by Hollywood standards. I'm a serial monogamist in both my marriage and work. While I've had a brush or two with death, I've been lucky enough, thus far, to avoid wars, natural disasters, or dreaded diseases. I've experienced anti-Semitism and hate, but only in a manner that would have made millions of martyrs chuckle. Ironically, rabbis are somewhat immunized from the kinds of overt anti-Semitism that might infect other workplaces; because we are so identifiable, people are usually on their best behavior. I've had some vexing moments professionally that have tried my soul, but most of the crises I've faced would not have made the cut for your average Lifetime movie or Oprah interview.

But that's precisely my point. There is nobility in normalcy, especially in untethered times such as these. There is a gallantry in overcoming everyday challenges that cuts to the essence of what the ancient rabbinic sages had in mind when they rescued Judaism from the rubble and ashes of another crazy apocalyptic era 2,000 years ago.

As A. A. Milne taught every child equipped with a honey jar and an imagination, you don't need wizards and dragons and secret portals to Narnia to find adventure and purpose in a Hundred Acre Wood. The Milne quotes sprinkled throughout the book act as a unifying thread, a reminder that boring can be beautiful. With a nod to Benjamin Hoff's classic 1982 introduction to Eastern religion, *The Tao of Pooh*, one might call this sacred life-poem that I present here, "The Torah of Pooh." There's a lot of dignity to be gained in the drudgery of daily life, and in the counted days of a single well-lived life. Such a life is, in its distinct way, heroic.

I came into my profession with a great deal of ambivalence. But with all the bumps that have occurred along the way, the "what ifs" and excruciating moments, I can now say, unequivocally, that being a rabbi has helped me grow into a far better human being than I would have been otherwise; a far more caring person, more appreciative of the precious legacy that I've been charged to reenergize, and more amazed, every day, at the simple dignity and courage of people, great and small. My sacred work has enabled me to make a small difference in the lives of some, maybe even more than that, but it has undoubtedly enriched my own life to a far greater extent. Here I share some of that enrichment with you.

My journey has taken me from my hometown of Brookline, Massachusetts, to Brown University, where I majored in religious studies, a path that brought me closer to my own faith tradition; then to the Jewish Theological Seminary for rabbinic training and New York University for journalism, then professionally to Beacon, New York, then down the Hudson River to Peekskill, and finally to Stamford, Connecticut, where I've spent the past three decades at Temple Beth El, a progressive, inclusive, Conservative congregation that was, for me, a perfect place to unpack and stay for a decade or three.

When I left Peekskill, an artist presented me with a gorgeous, framed paper cut with the Hebrew line from Psalm 90, "Teach us to count our days that we may gain a heart of wisdom." I hung it on my office wall in Stamford and stare at it every day. If I've nothing else to share, let me share that lesson through the pages of this book. Count your days and make every day count. That's what I've tried to do.

I dedicate this book to my father, Michal Hammerman, who was one of the nation's most renowned cantors when he died suddenly of a heart attack at the age of sixty on New Year's Day, 1979. He saw me enter rabbinical school and then left us three months later. This book is in no small measure a chronicle of my struggle to fulfill this dangling relationship, a bond that was severed so abruptly before it had had the chance to truly form.

I also dedicate it to my mother, Miriam Hammerman, who, living into her mid nineties—the last three decades with one lung—taught me through her struggles how to cherish each moment of life. She passed away just as this book was being completed. Formerly a concert pianist, she treasured every breath just as she used to caress each key. The ravages of Parkinson's robbed her of her ability to make music, but not of her smile, which still flashed nearly every time I visited.

And now, as I have passed the age of my dad's passing, I can sense that mortality will not allow me unlimited opportunities to get this right. So, this attempt to reclaim my father's legacy leads me right back to his clarion call to me and the overriding theme of his life: Being a *mensch*.

As an aside, you may be wondering why the unusual punctuation for Mensch•Marks. For one thing, I wanted the word "*mensch*" to be singled out, as I hope it can become the next big Yiddish thing to enter the English vernacular, like "chutzpah (recently accepted into American English by Webster's)," "schlep" and "kvetch" (which memorably made it into the screenplay of *Norma Rae*), following in the footsteps of Americanized Yiddishisms that people no longer even realize were once Yiddish, like "klutz," "glitch," and "bagel." *Mensch* is essentially untranslatable and it's a word our culture needs, and it is my fervent hope that this book will go a long way toward naturalizing it as a full citizen of American English, where it currently is still branded as a foreigner, a loanword, by being italicized in some style manuals. *Mensch* needs to be trending, not just in Bar Mitzvah speeches and eulogies. It needs to become a thing.

Additionally, that raised dot has an interesting name in English. It's called a "middot," as in, "a dot in the middle." But in Hebrew, that word connotes God's thirteen attributes of love, the *middot,* and more generally, precisely the kind of ethical qualities that a *mensch* embodies.

An entire Jewish discipline, the aforementioned *Mussar*, has been built on the cultivation of these *middot* in our lives. For those who feel that religion has been rendered irrelevant—and especially those younger Jews who have fallen away from Judaism—there is nothing more germane, life-affirming, and profoundly useful than the *middot* conveyed in these life lessons. It was the founder of modern *Mussar*, in fact, Rabbi Yisrael ben Ze'ev Wolf Lipkin, better known as Rabbi Israel Salanter, who summarized the purpose of his discipline precisely as I wish to frame this book:

> *At first I tried to change the world and failed. Then I tried to change my city and failed. Then I tried to change my family and failed. Finally, I tried to change myself and then I was able to change the world.*

The guy outside the gates of Sodom could not have put it better.

Finally, since my job is not simply to share but to inspire, prod, and occasionally cajole (it's what we rabbis do best), as you enter this very personal accounting of mine, I hope you will take it as a stimulus to chronicle your own Mensch•Marks, the encounters that have molded your character and helped you to navigate your way through your own Wilderness, bringing you closer to living a life—a fully realized *human* life—in God's image.

PART ONE

Work and Worship

. . . In which I explore my sacred profession. "Work" has always meant something other than "daily drudgery" in Jewish tradition. From the earliest days of the Bible to the advent of modern secular Zionism, there has always been something sacred about the work we do. In fact, the Hebrew words for work are directly connected to the sacred. The most common term, avodah, *not only means "work," it also is the term used for the sacrificial rites followed in the days of the ancient Temple. Later, when the Temple was destroyed,* avodah *came to be associated with that which replaced sacrifices: prayer. Our work is nothing less than a supreme offering to God, whether one is a rabbi, minister, imam, doctor, or welder. I see my task as being analogous to that of the ancient biblical prophet, of whom Abraham Joshua Heschel wrote, "He is neither a singing saint nor a moralizing poet. His images must not shine, they must burn." Work and worship stand united, for one leads to*

the other; prayer leads to world-mending activity, and such activity engenders awe and gratitude. That should be the case for all work, but it certainly must be the case for my profession. It has been for me.

"People say nothing is impossible,
but I do nothing every day."

—A. A. Milne, Winnie-the-Pooh

Mensch•Mark 1

1985

A YOUNG RABBI

Are Exuberance and Wisdom the Product of One's Age?

For the first two millennia of the rabbinate, age was equated with wisdom and experience with respect. Everyone abided by Leviticus 19:32: "Stand before the gray haired one [your elder]." No longer. It's sad, and not just for elders. Back in 1985, I could sense this transition happening and gave expression to my feelings in the following article, appearing in The New York Times Magazine, *which forced me to question whether any age would arrive when I would feel completely comfortable in my rabbinic role. But my encounters with ageism enabled me to hone a broader message and dedicate my life's work to breaking down all stereotypes that hide the true essence of our humanity.*

I am twenty-eight years old and a rabbi. Had I chosen to be a gymnast or tennis player, I would be considered past my prime. As a lawyer or computer engineer, I would be reaching the peak of yuppiedom. In my own eyes, I fret at how quickly the years pass while I helplessly watch my youthful vigor recede.

And yet, when I walk into my office each morning, I feel like a seventeen-year-old walking into a bar, fearful that some hulk of a bouncer will appear to check me for ID. I am a child in a profession where life begins at sixty.

Being a rabbi at any age inhibits normal social intercourse; being a young rabbi compounds the problem acutely. I am an anomaly in a community where rabbis are expected to have gray beards and the all-knowing countenance of one who is nearing the end of life's tumultuous journey.

I know that I am not alone; in many fields it is not easy to be young. In the two years since my ordination, I have left many a hospital room wondering whether the patients give their young doctors the same incredulous looks they often give me. A thirty-year-old dentist tells me of the difficulties of starting a practice—he wonders whether people will be willing to entrust their sacred smiles to one so young. Another friend, a psychologist, labors to establish his professional reputation. I feel for him, as well as for all the young men and women who strain to reach the next rung on the corporate ladder, only to be quashed by someone older. I feel for those who fritter away a half dozen precious years of youth at prestigious law firms, only to find that no partnership awaits them.

And yet my own position is particularly awkward. The awkwardness goes beyond the fact that I address doctors and judges by their first names while they call me by my title even when they are four decades my senior. It reaches beyond the fact that I commonly marry couples much older than I or that some of the more grandmotherly types I come across like to pinch my cheek. Wherever I go age is an issue, for not only am I cursed by being young, I am cursed by looking young. When the author of Ecclesiastes wrote , "Rejoice, O young man, in thy youth," he was not speaking to a convention of young rabbis.

I can understand why many of my rabbinical colleagues and class-mates choose to pursue other advanced degrees before entering the pulpit, while others prefer to spend years of tutelage under the wings of established rabbis in suburbia. Some, like me, stand alone, unprotected, and uneasy, but most are located somewhere out on the prairie, plant-ing Jewish roots in places where most of the natives have never seen a rabbi before. But here I am, in a pulpit just a hop from New York, where people know what a good bagel—and a good rabbi—should look like.

If I seem overly energetic to my congregation, the quality is attrib-uted to my age. My rather too apparent self-respect is something, they say, that will diminish "when I know better." Occasionally I am seen as being manipulated by one congregant or another; I am said to be easy prey because of my lack of experience. At a recent wedding, the father of the bride told me that I look more like a bookie than a rabbi. I made light of it (neither job, I said to him, is suitable for a nice Jewish boy), but I was sensitive to the anxiety underlying his remark. He was giving his daughter away, and the man who was going to put the stamp of God on the whole enterprise could just as easily be standing next to her—except that he's much younger.

My congregants ask themselves: How can this rabbi be mature enough to comfort mourners when he hasn't known a lifetime of per-sonal grief? How can he advise parents about their children when he hasn't yet reared children of his own? How can he counsel troubled couples when he hasn't been married long enough to experience mari-tal strife? How can he represent us before God when he hasn't been through our suffering, when he hasn't seen what we've seen? Can a rabbi who is not battle scarred truly be a rabbi?

These anxieties have eased as the congregation has come to know me. But I'm not sure the congregants know that, if anything, I fear the consequences of too much experience. When I perform weddings, I want to sense the exhilaration I felt at my own. When I visit the sick or console the bereaved, I want to approach them, not as a trained professional, but as one who is in some way personally affected by their plight. I prepare for each funeral as if it were my first, for it was at my first that I was best able to share in the sense of raw, unadulterated grief that consumed the family.

It is sad that so many Jewish communities seem to insist that their rabbis shed their youthful innocence as quickly as possible, not understanding that once the innocence is lost, the childlike sense of wonder and basic human empathy so essential to the job are also left behind. Once the rabbi loses his exuberance, even the most vibrant of communities becomes threatened with a similar stagnation. Perhaps early career burnout would be less of a problem among rabbis—and other professionals—if they didn't feel compelled to spend the first half of their careers trying to look older and the last half striving to regain the vitality of lost youth.

Still, my congregation has been very good to me, and I can only be grateful that they had the courage to employ me. They understand that I occasionally like to wear jeans and I prefer Lionel Richie to Benny Goodman. And they are beginning to understand much more.

Many of them perceive that I am a rabbi precisely because I want to break down barriers such as the one I face: stereotypes that poison human relationships. As I see it, I am a spiritual leader simply because I want to refine my own spirit, to stretch myself, using the texts of my tradition for guidance and, in doing so, possibly to inspire others to do the same.

If I remain a rabbi long enough, perhaps I will see the stereotypes crumble, and maybe someday there will be no barriers to honest, unprejudiced human contact in my little corner of the world. Perhaps. But by then I will be collecting Social Security, soaking up all the honor that comes with turning gray, and casting nervous glances at the young, idealistic whippersnapper of a rabbi skipping up the road.

Mensch•Mark 2

1 9 9 2 , 2 0 0 1

GENTLEMAN'S AGREEMENT

How I Learned to Afflict the Comfortable and Comfort the Afflicted

One question clergy always face is how to balance the desire to change people with the need to accept them as they are. As I've grown, I've tended to lean more toward acceptance, not out of frustration for having failed to change people, but, paradoxically, through accepting that the only way to transform a group of people is by loving them unconditionally, without any expectation that they will change. When I've worked with younger rabbis, that's been the hardest part to teach them—the part they never taught us at the seminary. Most rabbis never learn this and end up miserable.

What follows are reflections on how I came to love the people of one of the wealthiest counties around not for what they have but for who they are. Ultimately, I was able to help them to change the culture, leading by example. But my first misstep was a doozy. To this day, a quarter of a century later, people still bring it up. Over the years I've learned how to massage my message while refusing to sacrifice my prophetic calling. And more than that, I've learned that while preaching from the pulpit is all well and good, a big hug goes a lot farther.

When I came to my congregation in Fairfield County at the age of thirty, I told the world, and even convinced myself, that it was not about the money. Clergy are as susceptible to social climbing as anyone, but the ladders we scale tend to be ones of academic merit or denominational clout. So I came to one of the wealthiest counties in the nation not because I wanted to be part of that culture but, so I said, because I wanted to reform it.

I wanted to make the land of the classic 1947 film *Gentleman's Agreement* (where Gregory Peck pretends to be Jewish while navigating the anti-Semitic country-club world of Darien) kinder and gentler, to loosen the ties of the CEOs and replace their dry martinis with Manischewitz, to melt the icy quietude of their worship and shake up their Stepford conformity. It is interesting to note that Ira Levin, author of the 1972 novel *The Stepford Wives,* later told the *New York Times* that he based the town of Stepford on Wilton, Connecticut, where he lived in the 1960s, which he considered a "step" from Stamford, which sits fifteen miles away. Those were the days before the Merritt Parkway became so clogged that during rush hour that step has been lengthened considerably, but back then, Stamford Jewry was always just a step away from acceptance into the WASP bastions that would not let them in.

Now that I look back, I honestly think I really wanted to help change the culture of Fairfield County. But that's not why I came to Connecticut.

I came here to climb with the rest of them. Otherwise, why didn't I turn my head in disgust when someone boasted that the congregation had "dozens of millionaires"? Why didn't I just nod apathetically when informed of how, after morning services, one congregant would routinely exit our parking lot in a helicopter? Why didn't I scream in protest when, at my initial interview, one of the impeccably dressed questioners referred to my then place of employ as "blue collar"? Because in some manner, I was agreeing—and climbing—just like them.

I knew that if I they saw me as a prime candidate, it was because I brought to the table things that went far beyond my Talmud skills. But if they wanted to hire me because I attended an Ivy League college and had written for the *New York Times* or because I wore Brooks Brothers under my prayer shawl, that was fine with me.

They hired me and we struck a "gentleman's agreement." They would elevate my lifestyle and I would validate theirs. All I had to do was confirm that God had indeed blessed this place and that together we had reached Canaan—New Canaan, at least. The key was that I not challenge the status quo because to do so would imply that something was *wrong*, and, with what people were paying to live here, there couldn't possibly be trouble in paradise.

I gleefully officiated at black-tie Bar Mitzvahs. Starstruck by the celebrities I met, I ran out to buy my own tux and looked forward to attending dinner after dinner, honoring the billionaire of the month. In a perverse way, I even enjoyed paying condolence calls; each home I visited was more palatial than the last. I got to perform weddings in elite Manhattan hotels and tropical resorts. I was welcomed into the posh Jewish country club. I rose to the presidency of the local interfaith organization. I bought a nicer car, began drinking lots of frothy coffee. I was keeping up with the Goldbergs, and then some.

Then I got greedy. I wanted to have it all: the lifestyle and a social conscience, too.

So one year on Rosh Hashanah, I stopped talking about how nice things are and suggested that the world—even here—could stand a bit of . . . *improvement.* The owner of a local supermarket chain had recently been convicted of massive tax evasion. I suggested that I personally would not feel comfortable going into that store for the coming year.

Within a day, the word was out all over town: "RABBI PROMOTES BOYCOTT." I had done nothing of the sort, but what this told me is that I had done something far worse: I'd broken the Agreement. I'd hit Fairfield County where it least likes to be hit: right in the 1040.

I got many letters of support, but the board was not happy. I sensed a little buyer's remorse, not regarding the supermarket, but their hiring of me. My predecessors had never challenged the status quo so brazenly. The High Holiday sermons had never been so . . . well . . . *controversial.*

In the words of journalist Finley Peter Jones (but later embraced by religious leaders), "My business is to comfort the afflicted and afflict the comfortable." People who had for decades settled deeply into their chairs for the sermon, finding comfort in oratory balm, were suddenly afflicted. I didn't understand that. The question wasn't my "right" to challenge them, especially since I wasn't suggesting that *they* boycott, only that *I* would feel uncomfortable going into the store. The issue at hand was that I was, in their minds, issuing a *"Thou shalt,"* when they had never heard anything but *"I'm okay. You're okay."*

Commandedness is a difficult concept for people who grew up hearing that a "mitzvah" is a "good deed" rather than a commandment. The Ten Commandments long ago became the "Ten Suggestions" for most American Jews.

What I didn't intuit was how important it is to convey my ideals not in the language of revolution or anger but rather in the language of love. You can still challenge people if that challenge comes from a place of acceptance, mutuality, and vulnerability. Instead, I was, in their eyes, recklessly threatening a precious status quo while jeopardizing the future employment of the chain's employees, as well as the hard-earned acceptance of Jews in Fairfield County. Despite outward appearances of success, the insecurities of the "Gentleman's Agreement" were at that time still very much embedded into their DNA. While it was my responsibility to afflict the comfortable, I also needed to recognize that even those who *seem* comfortable are, in fact, afflicted by their own demons—and they need comfort, too.

In the end, as I fulfilled my personal pledge to avoid the store for a year, I received a call from the CEO of the chain, who offered an olive branch—yes, he had heard about the sermon—and a tour. He also threw in some cornstalks for our synagogue's *sukkah*, a sin offering, which I gleefully accepted.

From this sermon I learned some important lessons about the power of the pulpit and the weighty significance of every word I utter. And I learned the most important thing of all: not to stereotype my congregants but to see in them reflections of the divine image, human beings, just like me.

Mensch•Mark 3

THE SANTA SUIT

Do the Clothes Make the Rabbi?

For the past several years, my congregation has served dinner at local homeless shelters on Christmas Eve, bringing cheer to the residents and a welcome night off for Christian volunteers. As a rabbi, I always look forward to this chance to transform the dreaded "December Dilemma" into a classic Jewish act of kindness, a mitzvah, by feeding the hungry and lifting the downtrodden. It's an indelible experience eagerly shared by my family. Paradoxically, it never feels so good to be Jewish as when we are helping others to find fulfillment in their Christianity.

Last Sabbath, our social action chairperson announced during services that we were lacking one major component of this holiday presentation: Santa Claus. How could we bring seasonal cheer to these homeless children without a visit from Saint Nick? "If anyone has ever harbored the secret fantasy of being Santa Claus," he said, "now is your chance."

I thought . . . Should I? Can I? Might I volunteer to be the one if no one else stands up to this challenge? Would not the commandment to help these people in their time of need find its ultimate fulfillment in this one grand gesture? The next day I made a passing comment to the organizer that I just might be interested.

Then I began to envisage the complications that would inevitably arise. I imagined a grand entrance—Santa with a yarmulke, carrying a menorah—and wondered who would be traumatized more, the homeless Christian children or my own two confused young sons. And then when Santa started to light the Hanukkah candles and sing the blessings in perfect Hebrew, what message would this send? Would the younger kids think that Santa is secretly Jewish—and even more secretly a *rabbi*? I had the same problem a few years ago when I came to services on the festival of Purim dressed as Barney the purple dinosaur, much to the disbelief of all the toddlers present. To this day many undoubtedly wonder whether their friendly TV hero is really their rabbi in disguise.

I carried the scenario further, imagining a front-page photo of Rabbi Claus in the local newspaper. I pictured the scene on Christmas morning at the breakfast tables of Stamford: assimilated Jews with Christmas trees in their homes poking their spouses at the breakfast table saying, "See, even the rabbi does it!" To those Jews who, in contrast, have become living anti-Christmas V-chips, filtering out all graven, needle-shedding images from their lives, I'd suddenly be public enemy number one, a half step to the right of the evil Antiochus. I imagined hordes of Christians adding the Hanukkah lighting to their Christmas ritual, saying, "Hey, if Santa does it, it must be okay." I pictured my own kids adding several pages to their Hanukkah list, knowing that they are now getting their gifts straight from the Man (and most likely wholesale). I imagined the Grinch, somewhere, smiling.

My little innocent desire to bring some joy to a few homeless kids suddenly was getting very complicated, like Nathan Englander's tale of "Reb Kringle," the Macy's Santa literally driven to madness by the December Dilemma.

So I decided not to dress as Santa on Christmas Eve. Neither, however, will I dress as a rabbi. Of course, I'll be wearing my yarmulke— but that's because I'm a Jew. But I'll leave the rest of my rabbinic outfit at the door, that holier-than-thou inflection that is so hard for all clergy to shed: the droopy walk that comes from having the weight of the universe on our shoulders and a tinge of fearful mistrust that steers so many Jews far from anything remotely Claus-like at this time of year.

I'll head to the shelter in the hopes that joy and love will emanate from my every pore, and I'll belt out "Jingle Bells" with Maccabean force. If I can do this, and if the residents respond in kind, no external trappings will be necessary. The only garb that will matter will be that of one clad in kindness, one human being reaching out to another, loving our neighbors as ourselves.

Mensch•Mark 4

RISING ABOVE
THE HATE

*How Being a Rabbi Has Helped Me
to Become a Far More Loving, Far More
Forgiving Human Being*

Late Friday night the phone rang. When the caller ID blinked "Stamford Hospital," I braced myself. It was the emergency room; a Jewish patient was asking to see a rabbi.

Rabbinic nightmare No. 1: an emergency on Shabbat.

With strict privacy guidelines in place, it's usually easier to find out which ballplayers took steroids in 2003 than for clergy to learn about hospitalized congregants, but when I asked for the name, the nurse told me. Hearing it, I paused then asked, guardedly, "Are you *sure* the family wanted you to contact *any* rabbi?"

It's a common name, and for the sake of confidentiality, I'll use the Talmud's version of John Doe and call him Plony.

Could this be *the* Plony, the former congregant who spent the better part of a decade trying to orchestrate my departure? When his efforts were thwarted, he left the congregation, but last I heard, the man still carries a bowling ball–sized grudge.

Nightmare No. 2: turning the rabbinic cheek.

After two decades, I'd like to think I've got a rock-solid connection with my congregation. But it's axiomatic that there will always be 5 percent who will simply never be satisfied. That's the number they gave me in rabbinical school, and it has borne out through my career.

Plony was in the top percentile of that 5 percent.

So I was faced with a dilemma. If I failed to respond, I'd be neglecting a human being crying out for care. But the shock of my unannounced appearance in the ER could well kill him.

I knew that the latest Middle East peace plan would have a better chance of succeeding than my pastoral efforts, but I leaned toward going. This was an opportunity to rise above old grudges, swoop in, and trigger a healing reconciliation. Maybe this time the spirit of forgiveness would prevail.

Rabbis tend to be very good at rising above things, and I've no doubt that my career choice has made me a more compassionate person and better disciplined Jew. I've learned that life is too short to allow old grudges to fester, even if at times I've been compelled to ward off unfair attacks on my integrity. Turning the other cheek is primarily a Christian notion, and at times I've had to fight back. But I've come to understand how not to sweat the small stuff, even if "small stuff" includes a trifling matter like someone wanting to send my family packing. That's just part of the very complicated nature of the relationship between rabbis and congregants.

An issue of the journal *Sh'ma* features an exchange of letters between a pulpit rabbi and a nervous college graduate contemplating a rabbinic career, fearful that it would be spiritually and socially suffocating.

I remember that angst. When I entered college, the last thing I ever expected to be was a rabbi. It was my worst nightmare. I had seen how challenging such an existence had been for my father, a cantor, and for my family: life in a fishbowl, scrutinized from birth, talked about in the aisles of Marshalls, a succession of Sunday outings sacrificed for someone's funeral.

I had heard it all. The rabbinate sends people to far-off places from which they never return. As people come to see you through the lens of their expectations, the rabbi and his family begin to conform, quite subconsciously, to those same expectations. Before long, they are trapped inside a funhouse mirror, becoming grotesque parodies of what they had hoped to be.

But it doesn't have to be that way.

I echo the sentiments expressed in Rabbi David Glanzberg-Krainin's response to the graduate:

> Rest assured, there are rabbis who inspire their congregants to grow as human beings and as Jews; rabbis who are authentic in their own struggles with the tradition and with God; rabbis whose families are healthy and intact and loving. There are good rabbis who love what they do; and there are rabbis who are simply counting the days until retirement.

Not only is it possible to survive in my profession, it is possible to grow—to be more authentic and loving precisely because of all the spiritual tests we face. Not a day passes when I don't feel grateful for the trust my congregants have placed in me and for the responsibility I bear. I know that, to a degree, the future of the entire Jewish enterprise rides on every choice I make. To some, that burden is a nightmare.

But I wouldn't have it any other way.

That's what I was thinking as I held the phone in my hand. A human being was calling out for help, and somehow the call had come to me.

Yes, Plony's a jerk. But I answer to a higher authority.

I said to the nurse, "Um . . . is a family member there?'

"Yes. A son. Noah."

"Noah!"

I can't tell you the son's real name, but suffice to say that my Plony has no son with that name. Wherever Plony was, I now knew where he wasn't.

I spoke with Noah for some time, assisting him through the array of dilemmas he was facing. Fortunately, his father's condition was stable and there was no need for me to rush to his bedside. So everyone got a reprieve last Shabbat: both Noah and my own kids got to spend more precious time with their respective dads.

Mensch•Mark 5

SATURDAY MORNING FEVER

I'm Sick. Should I Hug the Bat Mitzvah?

I really do think a direct historical line can be drawn connecting the world's two oldest professions. My job, after all, is to touch people's lives, and touching is seen as a prerequisite to being fully human. But we live in a germophobic age.

I am not a prostitute.

That Nixonesque disclaimer was necessary to start because I now must point out that I am—and to be a competent clergyperson I *must* be—something almost as notorious. Yes, I am a proud member of the world's *second* oldest profession, a vocation that requires nearly as much on-the-job intimacy as that older one. Both professions stretch back to cultic origins and draw upon our innate craving to consummate bliss through human attachment, one through eros and the other through faith. When people in the hospital hold hands with their clergy, they feel the love of God, and that very touch can heal them. We have the power to wipe away loneliness with one simple stroke or pat—and we get paid to do it.

Never was this clearer to me than at a Sabbath service in 1997. My two young children had come down with the flu the previous weekend, so I was not shocked when, a couple of days later, I was shivering in bed with a personal-best fever of 103.7. On Tuesday the rabbi got sick. Four days later, with my temperature still soaring and a big Bat Mitzvah looming, I was sweating over one question alone: When the big moment arrives, how close should I get to the student?

This was not merely a question of propriety. For I am the healer, the hired conduit, and my illness was threatening to sever that divine connection. What's worse, the healer would be exposed as being merely human—and worse still, contagious.

Gone are the days of guilt-free sickness. Now the world fears illness and chastises the ailing. Dr. Mom has become Inspector Mom. Because I was too sick to return most calls, I had programmed my voice-mail with a phlegmy greeting informing people of my affliction. Big mistake. During the week, I had listened to seven consecutive messages beginning with, "You mean you didn't take the flu shot?" As the days passed, the remarks kept coming, boring harder and deeper with each beep, like a dentist's punitive drill slamming down into bedrock for traces of forbidden saltwater taffy. How could you? How dare you? To be sure, many also expressed get-well wishes, but while I was longing for the maternal caress, they were the ones acting as if the primordial parent had let them down.

I understood their sense of betrayal and began to blame myself. Everything that a rabbi represents to people was being challenged by my illness: defiance of mortality; stability in life's wild ride; the illusion of control. Since the days of Job, humanity's greatest defense against the inexplicable, utterly terrifying ways of God has been to concoct a human cause, inflict blame, and thereby manage the chaos. And when your spiritual leader is being punished for his sins, can anyone else possibly be safe?

As one who both preaches and practices greater intimacy in prayer, I spend more waking hours kissing (especially Torahs, holy books, phylacteries, and *tallit* fringes), and embracing people than do those of that more ancient profession. At the previous weekend's Bar Mitzvah, I had probably infected two or three hundred unsuspecting worshipers, who undoubtedly had gone on to spread the virus to thousands of others. But was I now supposed to recollect all my recent social encounters and inform each partner individually of my transgression? When every handshake becomes the moral equivalent of unprotected sex, are we heading quickly toward the elimination of all casual contact?

When the Israeli novelist David Grossman first visited America, he commented, "Americans are very polite, but trying to relate to them is like kissing through glass."

It's impossible to be a caring pastor without occasionally holding or shaking a hand, but more and more we are being asked to do our jobs with sterile gloves and masks. We've become so microbially beset that we've lost touch with touching.

I can see where this is heading. The Torah procession of the not-so-distant-future will feature the Bar Mitzvah student carrying the sacred scroll, followed by the glad-handing rabbi, cantor, and proud parents, then maybe a sexton, a synagogue officer or two, and finally, bringing up the rear, a member of the ritual committee dispensing gobs of Purell to the crowd.

Our society has become so obsessed with the violation of personal space that we've actually found an area where the doctors and lawyers agree. The medical profession is fixated on hygiene and the lawyers are loco about liability. Everyone is saying, "Hands off!" And because, sadly, a pastor's caring touch has all-too-often evolved into something more illicit, now even when that contact is totally well intentioned (as is the case 99.9 percent of the time), in this climate of pastoral paranoia it is often perceived otherwise.

At one time, the laws of ritual purity were more important than just about any other aspect of Jewish practice. An entire section of the *Mishna* is dedicated to them, focusing on impure vessels and food and the spiritual contamination caused by bodily discharges, corpses, and disease. One of the order's twelve tractates is called "*Yadayim*," or hands. But of these tractates, only one was considered relevant enough to warrant discussion in the Babylonian Talmud, the tractate "*Niddah*," which discusses a woman's menstrual cycle. Most Mishnaic purity laws were rendered obsolete by the destruction of the second temple in 70 CE; we recall them now with such acts as the ritual washing of hands before a meal.

The Psalmist equated clean hands and a pure heart (Psalm 24:4), and Rabbi Pinchas ben Yair was the first to liken cleanliness to Godliness (*Sotah*, chapter 9, *Mishna* 15). Did you know that God's ineffable name begins with the same letter—*Yod*—whose very name means "hand?" If you look at the most ancient proto-Semitic alphabet, the Yod looks just like a bent arm, complete with fingers. There is something very Godly about our hands—and there is no more sacred gesture than the human touch.

It is never easy to explain the laws of purity to modern Jews. Using the analogy of "cooties" makes it all seem so childish and shallow; these laws put us in touch with the deepest mysteries of life by constantly returning us to primal moments of passage, of birthing and dying. The ritual bath is enjoying a renaissance among even non-traditional Jews who are being awakened to that powerful experience of spiritual renewal. With each seepage of potential life (aptly called by

Rabbi Susan Grossman a "life-leak"), women and men are encouraged to replenish their pursuit of a life-affirming sexuality through the act of immersion. Even the most secular person—basically, anyone who has ever taken a hot shower after stumbling out of bed—can sense the restorative powers of flowing waters.

And even the most assimilated family knows to place water on the doorstep when returning from the cemetery. Pouring water over our hands helps us to forge a passage, a birth canal, back from the abode of death to the realm of the living. Then, once we enter the house of mourning, we immediately perform another life-affirming act: we eat.

We can appreciate our ancestors' obsession with purity because it mirrors our own. This generation might be the most germophobic in history. Before Purell, there was Listerine, which in the 1920s practically invented the American aversion to bad breath. In fact, the pseudo-medical term "halitosis" was created in 1921 as part of a marketing campaign. Pfizer, the company that brought us Listerine and acquired Purell in 2004, clearly understands the trend. Listerine sales have increased by double digits over the past couple of years. Lots of new anti-germ products are flooding the market, including a portable subway strap to avoid contact with the metal one, an around-the-neck-air purifier, and "antiviral" Kleenex, designed to kill cold and flu virus on contact.

In fearful times like ours, when the most dreaded enemies are unseen, we naturally tend to shy away from contact with the unknown—or, for that matter, the known, since even our most intimate friends are inundated with millions of invisible enemies. Everyone—and everything—is tainted. I've even seen Hebrew-school kids scouring the yarmulke bin for head lice. The purity laws are Judaism's way of acknowledging this fear of the invisible and channeling it into life-affirming action.

So now, what do we do in a Torah procession when people are afraid to shake? Maybe a Purell dispenser is the answer. But at the same time, I will hope to remind people that each extended hand is guaranteed to be at least 99.9 percent pure: because embedded within it is the first letter of the name of God.

When I returned to services the following weekend, word of my fever had spread like, well, a virus. Circling the sanctuary with the Torah scroll, I felt increasingly isolated, as if quarantined like the lepers of Leviticus, or that boy in the bubble. From the start, kissing and shaking hands were out of the question; then vocal communication—no one wanted to be less than twenty feet downwind—then even eye contact became difficult. With people turning away in fear, how could I reach out and draw them in? If I could not be a conduit for connection, how could I serve them and help them serve God?

Then came the moment of truth. I normally embrace B'nai Mitzvah kids when I present them with their Bible. With my coughing a noticeable distraction, I imagined the hundreds present asking themselves, "Will he, or won't he? Could this monster have the chutzpah to endanger this sweet-chanting flower, this tiny, beaming innocent just entering the prime of possibility—and just hours away from an awesome party?"

As I prayed for strength, I began to understand that in my preoccupation over the cure, I had failed to seize the opportunity to heal. Immunity might be a necessity for politicians and prostitutes, but for clergy it is our most dangerous pitfall. For us to succeed we must above all be flawed and vulnerable, reaching out from a defiled, squalid place that only real people can understand. That is how good leaders, from Mother Teresa to Moses, have become hallowed healers. Moses reached out to save his sister Miriam, afflicted with leprosy, that most isolating of diseases, even though Miriam had been spreading malicious gossip against him. Others can take flu shots. Only such champions of the spirit can inoculate our communities from the loneliness and cyber-sterility that threaten us all.

Somehow, prostitutes notwithstanding, the rest of us need to be able to touch.

So, I took my prayer book and kissed it, and at my soft instruction she, looking far wiser than her years, took her new Bible and kissed it, and we stretched our arms so that my sacred words could touch hers and, through that textual caress, thereby purify that unholy space hovering between us, which exists within all of us.

Mensch•Mark 6

MENTIONING THE UNMENTIONABLE

Smashing Taboos and Sacred Cows

It is so easy for a rabbi to preach what people want to hear. That makes for a feel-good service and usually a nice payoff in fund-raising. But sermons should not be judged on audience approval. Our job is to shake, rattle, and roll.

Ah, summer's here: a time for relaxation and renewal. But for rabbis, there is always a dark tunnel looming at the end of our summer sunlight.

At least this year, mercifully, the High Holidays don't commence until September 24. Last summer, with the holidays beginning on Labor Day weekend, rabbis could be seen with notepads on the beach, scribbling sermons while ducking the waves. This year, there is plenty of time to select topics and develop themes. And fortunately, there are some decisions that are easy to make—which brings me to the List.

You probably can recall that time in the recent past when your rabbi gave a High Holidays sermon almost identical to the one given by your cousin Ethel's rabbi in Saskatchewan. Everything was the same—right down to that wretched joke about ten minutes in, the one with the punch line, "That's why they call them Lord and Taylor." Well guess what: We're all reading the same sermon prep materials, either in books we buy at conventions or pamphlets disseminated by various rabbinical and philanthropic organizations. We're also reading the same Torah, commentaries, and Talmud, and it would be pretty strange if our messages had nothing in common.

But what's more interesting is the way we also choose not to speak about certain subjects, without a single prompt from the outside. This index of unmentionables is never sent, it is simply understood, as if handed down in some unspoken Jungian manner from generation to generation. We never discuss the List among ourselves. We just know.

So here, as a public service and without further ado, is Hammerman's Top Ten List of sermon topics you will almost never hear on the High Holidays.

10) Emigration to Israel (Aliyah) as a serious option all American Jews should reflect upon regularly.

9) White collar crime, especially tax evasion, as a serious breach of the Torah's moral code.

8) What other movements offer that ours doesn't.

7) Fur coats (especially if it's in the thirties on Kol Nidre eve).

6) Words like "commandment," "duty," and "obligation."

5) The Messiah (Lubavitch congregations excepted).

4) How leaders are chosen in Jewish life.

3) The fact that our religion is not better, nor truer, than any other world religion.

2) The drastic measures that need to be taken to increase Jewish literacy.

1) Why so many good pulpit rabbis burn out so fast.

The List can be tailored to suit the taboos of each congregation. A rabbi at an LGBTQ synagogue, for instance, would be highly unlikely to extol the Christian Coalition for its support of Zionism, and a congregation that is identifiably right wing on Israeli matters is unlikely to hear accolades about the Palestinians. And we always tiptoe around things that Judaism might consider of ultimate significance and sanctity, but Jewish Americanism considers in bad taste, including bodily functions and sexuality, frank discussion of death, and the need to smash idols and question assumptions.

Face it. The High Holidays were P.C. long before political correctness was invented. As each community defines its values, each rabbi is expected never to question them, whatever they may be, or risk family security, professional advancement, everything. Yet the sermon has to sound challenging, or the rabbi is perceived as a leader who refuses to lead. The artistry, then, is to take a pro-choice congregation and motivate it toward being more pro-choice, or to discuss the tax evasion of others without coming too close to home, and to make all that sound like leadership. The goal is to be enlightening, informative, and erudite. But the waves one makes can't be any more threatening than the ones the rabbi dodged at low tide in August, or else.

Yet without true questioning of one's presuppositions, there can be no authentic soul searching and, ultimately, no repentance. Rav Kook wrote in "The Lights of Penitence," "As long as a person is being driven by the bad habits surrounding him, he is not so sensitive to his sins." Breaking bad habits can be excruciating; ask any former smoker or recovering alcoholic. If the goal really is for teshuvah (repentance and introspective return) to occur, then the holidays must be, by definition, uncomfortable. The sermons can't just sound challenging, they've got to shake, rattle, and roll.

Complicating matters, another role of the rabbi, especially on the Holidays, is to provide comfort. After a year on life's roller coaster, Jews see the High Holidays as a marker in time, a chance to regenerate one's connection to self, family, and community. That regeneration is also part of the process of teshuvah. So, what's a rabbi to do?

Here's an exercise I recommend for everyone—not just rabbis. Choose a quiet pre-Holiday setting, a weeknight class, or a Shabbat service. Then ask what your congregation's Top Ten Taboo List would include. What are the sacred cows that no leader of your group would dare challenge without significant risk?

Then challenge them.

If the discussion maintains the tone prescribed by our tradition: respectful, inquisitive, and without rancor or slander, you will find the experience liberating. Many of our sacred cows will stand up to the scrutiny, and this effort will only serve to intensify our commitment to them. But some taboos just might crumble under the pressure of our questioning. Either way, the group will be strengthened, and the High Holidays will fulfill their promise as a time of community building.

As I navigate the tides of Cape Cod this month, then return to reflect and write, I'll be cruising the frontier between solid ground and murky waters, ever-questioning whether to duck waves or make them. But through it all I'll remember that my job is not to create controversy for its own sake but to destroy castles in the sand. For with each smashed idol, the path to the true God will become less cluttered, and true teshuvah all the more possible.

Mensch•Mark 7

1996

DANCING SHEVA

Flowing with the Rhythms of Sacred Time

Here's a reminder for rabbis—and everyone—to be authentic: to ourselves, to our souls' rhythms, and to our children . . . and through it all to dance.

The prevailing myth that goes around about rabbis is that we are incredibly overworked and constantly running to hospitals, nursing homes, and federation meetings, all the while composing perfect sermons and returning calls and letters. People think we're obscenely busy. They are wrong.

It's worse.

I realized that when I looked on my dashboard the other day. Dangling there—in the car that still needs its October emissions inspection, the inspection I recalled while paying October's bills sometime in early November—was a partly wound cassette entitled "Time Management for Rabbis." I'd never found the time to listen to the whole thing.

Hillel said, "Don't say that when I have the time I will study Torah, for you will never have the time." Hillel was one '90s dude. Before I can even begin to dream of the "leisure" Torah study that Hillel prescribes, I have to prepare for Shabbat and for all the classes I teach. Alongside the Torah work, I have pastoral work: visits, calls, responses to cries of pain both actual and anticipated.

It's easy to put things off. I believe it was Hillel who said, "If not now, *later*."

Imagine a doctor who not only has to care for the patients who come to see him but must follow up on every single patient all the time. It's not quite that extreme, but I always have more calls to make and more that I wish I could make. If I don't follow up often, I know that, to a degree, congregants feel they are losing touch with much more than a mere caregiver. Like it or not, the rabbi's concern, and therefore the rabbi's time, is perceived as an indication of God's love.

And in the midst of all this is my family, for whom prime time must be dedicated. At my eldest's circumcision, I promised him that the family would always come first. I've kept that pledge reasonably well, though not without great anguish on everyone's part. There just isn't enough time to do all that I want to do.

Just as my world is beginning to spin out of control, I am stabilized by the realization that the spokes of my week radiate from a fixed center: Shabbat. Although Shabbat is the day when I work the hardest and am most governed by the clock (just ask the congregant who subtly taps his watch during late-running services), the day rejuvenates me by marking work's completion rather than its cessation. When the day is done and all the programming is behind me—a sumptuous meal, a great discussion, two namings, an *ufruf* (pre-wedding Sabbath celebration), and lots of intense community building—I sense that all my frenetic jousting with time might actually have amounted to something.

Shabbat breaks time down into palatable parts, each week becomes a chapter with a beginning and an end. And just when I begin to feel as pressed as that retired football player who used to be seen running through airports (whatever became of him?), I find inspiration in, of all things, a sublime Hindu symbol, the Shiva Nataraja. Shiva is the center of all activity, the culmination of endeavor. In the words of religion scholar R. C. Zaehner, "He dances in the sheer joy of overflowing power; he dances creation into existence."

Shiva is the King of Dance, often depicted in a state of absolute motion, with arms and legs contorted in all directions yet his expression is one of unfathomable serenity. With one leg he maintains complete balance while another flails, and his outstretched arms appear to be effortlessly lifting up the world, even as his prime function in Hindu myth is a destructive one. Like Shabbat, he ends the process of creation. Where creation stops, existence can begin, and restoration and renewal inevitably flow from that.

Shiva reconciles all opposites: male and female, creation and destruction, human and divine. Shabbat also can do that. Dance can do that, too.

Early this month, a Bat Mitzvah student who also loves to dance choreographed all the prayers of the service to the steps of modern jazz, ballet, and tap. As she pranced around in my office, displaying the real leaps of rapture that should accompany the *Ashrei* prayer (which is all about joy), I saw a prayer that had been utterly boring to her suddenly come alive.

A few days later I brought my three-year-old Daniel to morning services. Midway through the *Kedusha* (holiness prayer), he abruptly left our row and began running circles in the aisle, singing out letters of the *alef-bet*.

Embarrassed, I coaxed him back to his seat.

Later he told my wife, "Daddy didn't want me to dance at temple today."

It made me think of that Bat Mitzvah student and how we drain our kids of the passion, the pulp of prayer, and how only the lucky few survive to reclaim it when they are older.

It made me realize that we spend too much of our time sitting *shiva* and not enough dancing it.

Okay, so the Dancing Shiva is a graven image. Minor technicality. Dancing wasn't patented by the Hindus; not even Zorba has a monopoly on it. We Jews, although historically long on verbosity and short on choreography, have had our great Lords of the Dance as well, including Miriam, David, and a host of Hasidic masters, not to mention Tevye the Dairyman's various incarnations.

A neo-Hasidic revival is now cutting across denominational boundaries because the joyous dance of the Baal Shem Tov is just what our hassled masses are looking for. So what if most of us *shuckel* (the movement of prayer) with two left feet and can't do the Macarena with abandon?

We have been wallflowers for too long. It is through such movement that we can be released from time's shackles and begin to dance our way through airports and through life.

The Alexanderer Rebbe said, "We read in Isaiah 55:12, 'For you shall go out with joy.' This means: If we are habitually joyful, we shall be released from every tribulation."

So it's not the dancing we do on the dance floor that matters. It's the dancing we do in our hearts.

I've come to understand that it is far preferable to be hyperbusy than to have nothing important to do. If we can accept that we'll always feel the crying need for more time and that death will ultimately keep us from finishing the job, we can begin to know the satisfaction of filling each instant to the brim.

I don't need to manage my time according to a preset plan. Every moment I am leaping along the spokes of my Shabbat-centered wheel, chaotic yet balanced, flailing yet serene. I have not one second of free time, yet I feel totally liberated. No need to pace myself, nor could I if I wanted to.

I leap from spoke to spoke, day to day. There are seven days. In Hebrew, seven is *sheva*. After funerals, Jews sit *shiva*. But to be a Jew is also to be *dancing sheva* . . . and to be a wallflower no more.

Mensch•Mark 8

1996

SUPERRABBI, THE FLAWED MODEL

Taking Myself off the Pedestal

In an era of widespread sexual, financial, and power abuses by clergy, it has never been more important to stop deifying them. I write this in 2018, when, in the wake of #MeToo, the most prestigious megachurch in the United States, Willow Creek, has been rocked by a scandal including allegations of sexual misconduct by founding pastor Bill Hybels. Katelyn Beaty wrote on Religion News Service, *"The Hybels story is, of course, about sex—how sexual desire, left unchecked, damages relationships, marriages and entire ministries. But it is, at a far deeper level, about power: how individuals wield it and how institutions protect it. . . . Churches must seek leaders who are accountable and vulnerable, not just charismatic and driven." We clergy all need to get ourselves down from the pedestal.*

Item: A seventh grader's soccer coach has scheduled a practice for Rosh Hashanah. The girl walks up to the coach and says, "You'd better change this or my rabbi's gonna beat you up." She later relates the story to me, with a proud smile on her face. I pray that the coach is not a black belt.

Item: I am welcomed to a new congregation at a service filled with intense excitement and anticipation. The cantor dedicates a new musical composition in my honor, based on Isaiah, called "The Lord Is in Our Midst." I fret that expectations are running a tad high.

Item: A large influential group of Jews proclaims that their rabbi is the Messiah. The rabbi dies, but some insist that he is still the Messiah and will soon return.

The role of the rabbi has always been complex, but lately it appears to have broken the bounds of all human capability. There have been wonder-working rabbis for centuries, but none until now have been called upon to pull off the greatest miracle of all: to single-handedly fill the gaping spiritual hole in the postmodern, alienated Jewish soul. This is a job for Superrabbi.

Like frantic Lois Lanes falling from a burning building, people are reaching out—people without roots and without purpose, all stretching their arms toward Superrabbi to heal, to shepherd, and to redeem them. Skeptical people, betrayed by the very modernity that promised them salvation, now turn to this lonely man of faith, imploring, "Make my life full, before it is too late . . .

. . . only don't expect me to commit to anything."

. . . only I don't want my friends to see that I am vulnerable."

. . . and don't forget, it's because of you that I'm so alienated."

And who is "you"? "You" is what I've come to call the O.B.R., the One Bad Rabbi. All it takes is one and a Jew can be turned off to Judaism for life. Apparently, many Jews have had him or her, and all went to the O.B.H.S., the One Bad Hebrew School, where this O.B.R. used to rap knuckles and force kids to sing while screeching chalk along the blackboard with sadistic pleasure. Whatever this O.B.R. did, and it ranges from giving O.L.S. (One Lousy Sermon) to adultery, what matters is that he fell short of expectations and therefore so did Judaism. The O.B.R. is the one reason I hear more than any other for individuals having been turned off to organized Jewish life.

If the O.B.R. is so dangerous, it's because she or he is Superrabbi unmasked. If we were not to rely so heavily on Superrabbi to save us, we'd be far less susceptible to the inevitable revelation that rabbis are fallible. Judaism is too important, and its future too uncertain, for Jews to place its fate in the hands of a single human being.

Or maybe the O.B.R. is just a convenient excuse for those who long ago left the fold but don't want to blame the other likely culprits: Mommy and Daddy, conformity, greed, fear, and self-hatred. Whatever the reason, the O.B.R. has got to go and Superrabbi with it.

Through the ages, Jews have had a knack for creating the perfect model of leadership to match their needs. In ancient Israel, kings and prophets answered the call for military might and social justice. In Babylonian exile and beyond, prophets became more comforting and priests arose to create the rituals that would bring the people back into God's favor.

Then in the wake of the Second Temple's destruction, the rabbinic model of scholar, arbiter, teacher, and part-time miracle worker came to dominate the Jewish world. The source of his power was clearly his ability to reason. In the melting pot of twentieth century America, the rabbi was converted from teacher to pastor-shepherd so he could be just like the Christian clergy next door but with all the ancient Jewish trappings of the miracle worker intact. When the holy man is a teacher, his holiness endows him with wisdom, but otherwise he remains human; when the holy human is primarily a pastor, however, her mere touch can bring salvation.

That kind of promise arouses superhuman expectations—and disappointments.

Further, if the rabbi is a shepherd, that makes the rest of us sheep. Okay, so Moses, David, and Rabbi Akiba started out as shepherds, but they didn't have to worry about a soaring assimilation rate. If the rabbi is a shepherd, he has to lead the flock up the hillside, pulling, pushing, and cajoling. Superrabbi is expected to get those sheep to the destination, even if they don't want to go.

I have a better idea. How about the rabbi as a cotraveler, a very well-educated member of the flock? I chose this model for myself long ago. I don't push or pull my companions. I share my experiences and learn from theirs. Together we strive to reach the thick pasture at the top of the hill.

I believe that the rabbi is neither holier than others nor less human. The extent to which the rabbi can share humanness, in fact, is the extent to which he can touch the lives of those who choose to travel along. To be the "perfect rabbi," therefore, is not to avoid mistakes but to make them and then grow from them.

It is time to reaffirm the original intent of the rabbinic model as teacher and spiritual guide in order to rescue our communities from the ravages of unmet expectations.

It's clear that if we are to navigate our way through this crisis in confidence and reestablish the rightful place of the rabbi in Jewish life, we have to both safeguard the integrity of the role and reaffirm the frailty of the human being who fills it. And that begins when the rabbi steps down from the pulpit of the soul and laughs, cries, errs, and repents together with the rest of us. In the end, it doesn't really matter how the rabbi is addressed. What matters is only *that* the rabbi is addressed, one soul to another, two flawed human beings in dialogue.

If Superrabbi is allowed to survive, we're setting ourselves up for a fall. In the end, we will be left with only burned-out rabbis and dissatisfied congregants, lots of O.B.R.s, and very few Jews.

Mensch•Mark 9

SHEDDING THE BAGGAGE

Baring My Soul Before God

I know of a rabbi who said at his retirement that he hadn't prayed for forty years. He'd been so busy orchestrating the choreography of prayer that he forgot to leave time for his own spiritual growth. Such is the fate of one who allows the ballast to grow unchecked, the schmutz, the layers of accumulated stuff that always gets in the way. That's what happens after three decades as a religious professional. As the subtitle of this book indicates, religion offers needed ballast in untethered times. But excessive grounding can leave us spiritually grounded. That's why I constantly need to scrape off the barnacles that cleave to my soul.

Have you ever stopped to think of how many useless things you've accumulated? The festival of Sukkot (Tabernacles) is a great time to reflect on this as we recall our ancestors' journeys through the

Wilderness with few possessions but enormous faith. This realization also hits me when I head to the outlet malls to buy the exact same khaki pants I purchased a few years before—only one size larger. I buy the new pants reluctantly but simultaneously pledge not to part with the old pair, just in case. The Messiah will undoubtedly come before I again fit into them, but I keep the older apparel nonetheless. I hate to throw things away.

It's the same with magazines. In my basement I have decades of *Newsweek*s and *Sports Illustrated*s (worth pittance compared with all those baseball cards my mother chucked), and a few ancient copies of the *Jerusalem Post* when it was left-wing. And then there's my fourth grade math homework, my old harmonica, some Hebrew notebooks with all the original psychedelic *alef-bet* doodles, and letters—loads of letters: personal, junk, and life-transforming . . . enough mail to fill the Smithsonian someday after I write the great American-Jewish novel, follow up with my memoirs, and die.

But in the unlikely case that I don't become obscenely famous, I have to start lightening the load.

Baggage accumulation, like the national debt, rises uncontrollably even as we seek to rein it in.

Every Passover, I dutifully perform the ritual of spring cleaning, but with each Seder comes another albumful of snapshots, accompanying the escalating collection of clippings for the files, books for the shelves, videos for the cabinet, CDs to replace the tapes to replace the LPs to replace the 45s to replace the 78s, to put next to the 486 to replace the 386 to replace the PC Junior to replace the slide rule. If I were to sit down and read all the books stacked in a neat pile on my night table, I'd never have the time to scan the millions of pages of literature I can download right now from the internet or onto a CD-ROM. It is petrifying to note that through computer technology I now have access to a Judaic library greater than the cumulative libraries of all the great and not-so-great sages of the last 2,000 years. This baggage has deep value, but one can suffocate from the sheer weight of it.

Judaism has lots of baggage, too. Our core acts of religious expression have been smothered by centuries of accumulated embellishment. Though some *piyyutim* ("religious poems") are beautiful, most come across now like the old clothes that fill my closets. Very few of them actually "fit," and by the time you get around to the best stuff, you're too tired from trying them on to notice.

But we keep adding layers to the point where our prayer shawls are becoming as weighty as those spacesuits worn by the astronauts. As I stand during the *Amida*, the central prayer of the service, straining to lift myself to angelic heights with each utterance of the word *Kadosh* ("Holy"), I am weighted down by so much ballast that it is virtually impossible to pray.

Maimonides wrote about twenty-four things that keep us from true repentance. Umpteen impediments keep me from truly baring all before God each moment of each day. If the world is a very narrow bridge, as Rabbi Nachman of Bratzlav suggested, then in order to cross it we must cut loose the loaded U-Haul we are dragging along. The problem is that the things we jettison might prove valuable to others, including our own children. So we shouldn't obliterate everything; rather, we should place the superfluous in storage—somewhere else. Then, free at last, we can begin to navigate that narrow bridge.

So what could we do without? What weighs us down? For one, we really don't need cable news. Try going without it for a week and we might discover something amazing: our own opinions. On a Jewish communal level, we probably have a few too many organizations and far too many fundraising dinners. We really don't need so many added festival days in the Diaspora, and we could cut down on the times we repeat certain prayers at services. We could do without lengthy sermons and excessive musical solos, too. But these aren't really what weigh us down.

Our primary burdens are self-inflicted. They include feelings of guilt and inadequacy; unresolved relationships with parents, children, spouses, and lovers; and hopelessness. The burden comes not from accumulated photos and fourth grade homework but from seeing those bygone days as our best days.

Then there are the burdens of pretension, status seeking, and conformity. The obsessive fear of change is a horrible burden to bear, as is the need to always be right. Hatred is equally terrible, taking so much energy to sustain.

When we shed all these burdens, the other trappings hardly matter. So what if there are three daily services, five black-tie dinners, and a closet full of outsized pants? These are the peripherals. The junk I schlep from place to place can often spring to life with new, sudden significance if only I could color them with hope and humility.

If only I allowed myself to shed the extraneous layers and bare my soul before God, not allowing anything to get in the way, not the page number I have to announce next or the name of the collation sponsor. Then I would truly be God's instrument, a violin in God's hands, allowing myself to share my most beautiful music with God's world.

I *am* God's instrument, exposed and lithe. And all the old pictures, the extra prayers, and ancient periodicals serve to moisten the strings when I myself am stored away for the night. Even my old harmonica has become a life-giving force; it is the instrument of an instrument. These things can easily accompany me across that narrow bridge not as the ballast but as the bounce.

If only I could let the baggage go.

PART TWO

Loving and Letting Go

. . . In which my private and public roles intersect in the challenges of family life. At his Bar Mitzvah, my son Ethan stated, "I'd like to thank the rabbi. He's been like a father to me." That line, funny as it was (it brought down the house), demonstrates the fragile balance that must be struck between private and public. This has always been true for clergy, but now, given the decimation of privacy, particularly in social media, it's true for everyone. Long before Facebook my family's life was already an open book because any rabbi who is modeling how to be fully human, any leader who hopes to be fully present and authentic, needs to share these most human experiences. At the same time, we need to instill clear boundaries, which I've tried to maintain.

If you live to be a hundred,
I want to live to be a hundred minus
one day so I never have to
live without you.

—A. A. Milne, Winnie-the-Pooh

My father was God and didn't know it. He gave me
the Ten Commandments not in thunder and not in anger,
not in fire and not in a cloud, but gently
and with love. He added caresses and tender words,
"would you" and "please." And chanted "remember" and "keep"
with the same tune, and pleaded and wept quietly
between one commandment and the next . . .

. . . Then he turned his face to me one last time,
as on the day he died in my arms, and said, I would like to add
two more commandments: the Eleventh Commandment,
"Thou shalt not change,"
and the Twelfth Commandment,
"Thou shalt change. You will change."

—Yehuda Amichai (from the poem, My Father's Lodging Place,
from his collection, *Open Closed Open*)

Mensch•Mark 10

FATHERS
AND SONS

The Power of Parental Presence

The birth of my first child brings me full circle, back to the scene of my father's death.

What I'm going to write here will sound sexist to some, but I beg my female friends to indulge me on this one. My training in religious traditions makes me take special note of the unique complexity of the father-son relationship. For Jews, the primary command of the Passover Seder is to tell the story to your son (which in many modern translations has been expanded to include daughters, too). In Islam, the Quran is to be memorized and recited, with special care given toward its transmission to sons. And for Christians, the story of Jesus revolves around the most theologically complex father-son relationship imaginable—complex yet so very simple.

For it all comes down to one thing: every son needs a father, a close father to love and teach him, one who is present and caring, whether the father be the simplest of men or God.

My father collapsed from a heart attack on New Year's Day 1979, during halftime of the Rose Bowl. That's when my mother called me from Boston and I began the longest and most difficult journey of my life. I was a first-year rabbinical student living in New York at the time, four hours from home, four hours from the finality that in my heart I suspected was coming. Although my mother's words told me that he was still alive, her voice hinted at a more devastating truth. But that truth remained as elusive as the road beyond the reach of my headlights on that rainy night, and time stopped for me while I made that nonstop drive.

I turned onto my street and saw from half a block away that all the lights were on in my house and at least a dozen cars were parked outside. Not a good sign. A darkened house would have meant everyone was still at the hospital, where there might be some hope; but no such luck. The choice was mine: go inside and face the irreversible void that was about to enter my life, or drive on in the hopes of keeping time frozen indefinitely—as if once or twice around the block would change everything back to normal.

Fast-forward twelve years, to the birth of my first child, Ethan. With my wife about to deliver, I felt myself turning the corner of that street once again. And then, when Ethan was pulled from his mother's womb and his face turned toward me, I knew that my eons of roaming aimlessly around the block had ended. My father had returned.

The face was too serious and calm to belong to an infant, and too focused on one object in the room: me. It was as if those eyes were imploring me that it was now okay to leave the car and come into the house. The hair, the lips, the nose, they belonged to Ethan, but the eyes were my father's eyes. And in a single moment, the distant past became the present, from death came new life, and the clock that had stopped so abruptly that New Year's Day began ticking again. Halftime was finally over.

My dad was a rarity for his era, demonstratively affectionate and involved with his children, day and night. Unlike all those TV daddies of the Ward Cleaver era, mine actually took me to his office—often. (And how often did Fred and Barney take Pebbles and Bamm-Bamm to the quarry?). While he worked, I filled coloring books and traded knock-knock jokes and corny riddles with the secretaries.

In *Iron John*, Robert Bly writes of the phenomenon of the remote and absent father, so pervasive during the past three decades. This is the dad so often mocked in our popular culture, the one who has no idea which cold remedy to take and where the diapers are hidden. Even the success of the "sensitive dad" films like *Mrs. Doubtfire* or *Mr. Mom* only served to reinforce the notion that authentic, all-American dads aren't supposed to be involved with their kids unless they get fired, and the only way to be a good, caring dad is to be a mom in disguise.

Citing the work of a German psychologist, Bly argues that if the son does not actually see what the father does during the day, a hole will appear in his psyche, "and the hole will fill with demons who tell him that his father's work is evil and that the father is evil." It was the absent father of the Ward Cleaver era that led directly to the student protests of the '60s, Bly suggests, as the students' fears regarding their own fathers were transferred to all male figures in authority.

I don't want to be a Mr. Mom. I want to be a Mr. Dad, but one whose son will never feel that his father has abandoned him. I want to be a present father. When the boy cries, I want to hold him every time until the cry becomes a coo. And if that is impossible, which it is, I want him to have such vivid memories of me that he'll feel me there even when I'm not. The father who is present to his child is never remote, I've discovered, and the father who is remote is never present, even when he is in the same room.

What Passover and Easter share, I believe, is the idea that even when a present father appears to be off on an endless business trip, he can still hear and be heard. What those sibling holidays teach us is that the loving parent never really dies and the loving God always returns. We wait. But the Israelites waited, too, through centuries of toil in a far-away land, and I waited for twelve years before an answer finally came.

For twelve years I had been continually driving around that block, refusing to allow myself to be drawn into the light of my home, to the finality of my father's death. For twelve years I had been orbiting. For twelve years I had been searching for my father, and in one magical instant I found him.

In the book of Genesis, Abraham's words to Isaac were never recorded, but between the lines of the text one can guess what must have been said by one about to die at the hands of his father. Isaac's silent scream was a cry filled with the horror of the ultimate parental abandonment, one equaled in intensity only on rare occasions through-out history—perhaps only in Egypt or at Golgotha. Or in Auschwitz. "My God, my God," echoed the pleas of the enslaved Israelite, the suffering Jesus, and the brutalized European Jew. "Why have you forsaken me?"

These cries to a common Father were often heard—and often not. Many of us are still waiting.

Meanwhile, I discovered something quite astounding in February 1991. My father was back, all right, but he could no longer be detected in the face of my son, though those eyes did continue to look strangely familiar.

Instead, my father chose a most curious yet appropriate place to make his presence known: in my own presence. Inasmuch as Ethan's dad has been able to be the kind of present father every child deserves, a child of any age, Ethan's grandfather will never be very far away.

Mensch•Mark 11

THE DANGLING KNIFE

The Parent as Sculptor, Mentor, and Shield

As one of their duties, rabbis guide nervous parents through the ritual wounding of their son's genitalia on the eighth day following birth. I've led hundreds of mothers and fathers through their baby boys' circumcisions, reciting my routine explanations in favor of the ritual. But it was not until the birth of my younger son, Daniel, that I came to appreciate the deeper meaning behind circumcision. True, I had witnessed hundreds of cuttings, but until that day I had never myself performed one.

As a rabbi and as a parent, I had figured that my second son's circumcision would be like that of the first. I assumed I would chant a blessing or two, then daub his mouth with wine-soaked gauze. But the mohel (circumciser), Dr. Harry ("Hesh") Romanowitz, with whom I had worked countless times, suddenly handed me the knife. He pointed to my squirming child, whose hands and legs were tied to the board. The foreskin had been pulled up over the glans of the penis and was now protruding through a narrow slit of the small, stainless steel clamp.

"It's all set up," the mohel said. "No way you can go wrong."

"It's the greatest honor a father can have," he added.

He had taken that line right out of my script. But there was one difference: I remind parents that they have the option of delegating to the mohel the performance of that radical affirmation of the covenant between the Jewish people and God.

"All you have to do is cut," he said.

Daniel, who had been crying incessantly throughout, suddenly stopped. Like Isaac centuries before, Daniel waited in silence for his father's knife to drop.

Daniel had spent most of his first week of life blissfully attached to one or the other of my wife Mara's breasts while I played computer games with two-year old Ethan. I also attended to the medical insurance, informed relatives of Daniel's birth, got his Social Security number, and shopped for food. In short, I had become Master of the Mundane—until I was handed the knife.

Since the day Abraham circumcised Isaac, the knife has transformed father into sculptor, asserting his responsibility to mold and perfect nature. The knife also turns father into mentor, one willing to inflict pain for the sake of proper moral development.

But most of all, the knife turns father into potential murderer. It is no coincidence that only one biblical chapter after Abraham circumcises Isaac, he nearly slaughters him, perhaps with the same knife. One does not have to be a Freudian to know that the birth of a son brings about more than unalloyed joy to the father. There is no greater primal anger than that caused by seeing another male in carnal contact with your wife, in this case the physical intimacy of mother and son. And there is no greater primal envy than that caused by looking down at the person who was brought into the world specifically to be your survivor. In traditional Jewish society, a male child is called a *kaddish*, the one who would say the memorial prayers when the parent dies. With the birth of a *kaddish*, the father hears a whisper that it is now all right to die.

In the face of this anger and jealousy, give the father a knife and ask him to do *that*? *There*? And besides, I'm squeamish. The last time I gave blood, I passed out. I shave only with an electric razor. I'm a vegetarian. And finally . . . well, let's just say that I am no surgeon. Mara and I ruminate for hours before cutting our baby's fingernails. But with our friends and relatives waiting impatiently, what was I to do when the mohel handed me the knife? I took it in my right hand, forgetting that I bat, throw, eat, and probably cut foreskins best lefty, and swallowed hard.

My hand trembled as I began to push the blade across the edge of the clamp through which an inch of my infant's foreskin protruded. But the blade wasn't cutting easily. The seconds felt like hours as my hand swayed back and forth.

The situation called for a hard, sturdy chop. It called for a butcher. In fact, in the Middle Ages, the community's mohel was often the one who slaughtered animals for kosher meat. Looking at my son, I realized success required tunnel vision, to regard the skin as lifeless, distinct from the person attached to it. But I wasn't used to cutting meat, raw or cooked. Was this what it was all about? Unprovoked aggression? Dehumanization of one's own flesh and blood? It was becoming clear that in order to finish the job I would have to rely on a carnivorous side that I didn't think existed, that I feared greatly.

Then Daniel began to cry again.

I suppose that had Abraham fumbled things this badly; even stoic Isaac might have cried. But Daniel let loose a wail that normally was reserved for four in the morning and was always assuaged by a speedy rendezvous with his mother. This time, though, it was just the two of us. I was holding the knife, and he appeared to sense its power.

Then I noticed for the first time his blue eyes looking straight into mine, and it was a look not of fear but of utter dependence and trust. It was the kind of look we Masters of the Mundane aren't used to getting from infants.

I finally understood that the knife transforms the father not into sculptor, mentor, or butcher but, paradoxically, into a shield. The breast provides but the knife protects. It channels a father's natural anger and jealousy into one controlled cut. He takes off one small part in order to preserve—and love—the whole.

A rush of guilt and fear went through me. I just wanted to hold Daniel and tell him that never again would he suffer the agony of rampant parental rage. With one burst of empathy and a series of short jagged flicks, the foreskin was gone. The mohel cleaned things up and it was over.

No parent should be denied this experience, even vicariously, of inflicting upon his child a ritualized blow so intense as to make him both shake and recoil, yet so controlled that no damage is really done, to signify that this will be the worst the child will ever know from his parent's hand. For it is from the father's hand that Abraham's knife dangles every moment of every day.

Mensch•Mark 12

2006

HUGGING, BLESSING, LETTING GO

With Every Embrace There Must Be a Release

As a Bar Mitzvah approaches, the mohel's slicing is replaced by some serious molting, providing a lesson in peeling off.

One morning my son Dan came to breakfast with a subtle rasp in his otherwise crisp, cherubic voice. Normally that would not be a big deal, but with his Bar Mitzvah just weeks away, every minuscule vocal deviation was a major concern.

The human body virtually reinvents itself every day, replacing billions of dead cells, especially on the skin. But a voice change, like the Bar Mitzvah itself, is among those landmark events that register most profoundly on the parental Richter scale. These past few months, similar no-turning-back events have been occurring in my household with alarming frequency. Dan had gotten braces a couple of months before,

I got stronger glasses, and not long after that, I gave my other son, Ethan, nearly fifteen, his first shave.

I've always believed in hands-on parenting. Thirteen years before, I had performed Dan's circumcision. And as I navigated my Norelco Tripleheader down Ethan's chin and across his stretched neck, gingerly sidestepping the Adam's apple and juking the jugular, I noticed some real similarities between the two cuttings. Sometimes the blade is necessary, but no parent wants to apply a blade to any child, anywhere, at any time. Aside from not wanting to cause pain, I shuddered at being a participant in such a miraculous molting, peeling away at the layers of the boy only to reveal the man. The blade only tickled Ethan. I was the one feeling diced.

I shaved him knowing that the alternative would be to let him do it himself, something I had tried on my own teen face nearly a lifetime ago, leaving it looking like the West Side highway after a late winter thaw, littered with scrapes and potholes. So I sheared him, and then again and again, awed each time not only at my holding over him the power of life and death, but that with each stroke I was midwifing his rebirth into adulthood and my own into obsolescence.

It is petrifying to be a parent, so much so, in fact, that since the Middle Ages, Jewish parents of a Bar Mitzvah have recited the oddest of blessings. It reads: "Praised is God, who has relieved me of guilt for whatever becomes of this child." Historians trace this *Baruch Shep'tarani* blessing back to the biblical story of Jacob and Esau, brothers whose post-adolescent lives took dramatically different tracks. Although Rebecca and Isaac were hardly exemplary parents, the blessing validates their unavoidable helplessness in opposing Esau's wayward ways. In instituting this prayer, the rabbis were implying that there comes a point where parents simply have to let go.

Even as my kids are now young adults, I have a lot of trouble doing that.

I live with the dread every day, aware that each letting-go is a dress rehearsal for the ultimate Letting-Go. I know that when I die, my children's first act will be to consummate that separation with the ritual cutting of clothing, every bit as painful as the circumcision and shaved chin, and every bit as necessary for further growth.

Everything happening now is leading up to my being left in the dust. First they crawl, then walk, then ride a bike, then drive a car. The speed increases with each new step, all the while nature is taking its entropic toll on the parent huffing and puffing behind, falling away like the spent first stage of a Saturn 5. With each passing milestone, my ability decreases to ensure their survival—and my own.

I remember exactly when Ethan's math homework became too tough for me, and I recall my embarrassment at discovering that what used to be considered R-rated is now being packaged as PG. *Meet the Fockers* was an education for all of us. But still I hold on to their childhood for as long as I can, for as long as they will let me.

As a rabbi who has served the same community for nearly a generation, I feel like I've said *Baruch Shep'tarani* hundreds of times as week after week "my" children have paraded across the pulpit and out into the world, slipping beyond my grasp into adulthood. But there is no *Baruch Shep'tarani* for clergy, however, or, for that matter, for God. Only parents can love children enough to let them go.

Ethan may unwittingly have been speaking for all my other students when, at his Bar Mitzvah, he got up before a packed congregation and said, "I'd like to thank the rabbi . . . he's been like a father to me." I may have shaved only him, but as the kids come and go, I feel like I've been shearing the entire flock. I cut; they run.

These ruminations were just a preview of the real moment of dread: Dan's Bar Mitzvah. I stood at the Torah and watched Dan ascend, my baby in his fresh-cut suit, looking and sounding like a burgeoning man, with the deepening voice, the braces, and the first hint of adolescent blemish on his smooth, dimpled face. I whispered a measured *Baruch Shep'tarani*, cleared my throat, and in a raspy, broken undertone let him know how proud I was.

And another layer of my adult skin slid away. Only part of me survived this ordeal: the part that has learned how to hug with one arm and let go with the other.

Mensch•Mark 13

LEAPING WITH ANGELS

My Sick Child, My Dying Congregant, and Salvation from an Unexpected Source

Morris Margolies wrote about Jacob's ladder in his book *A Gathering of Angels: Angels in Jewish Life and Literature*. He tells us, "Life is two-directional. Its valleys are as normal as its peaks, its defeats as frequent as its triumphs . . . If you have faith that God is by your side wherever you are, and that even when you hit the bottom rung of the ladder, you are still in the company of angels."

According to the great Hasidic Rebbe of Kotzk, God fashions a ladder from heaven to earth and sends people down at the time of birth and the whole idea of life is to climb back up that ladder. But what happens is that after we climb down, God pulls the ladder back up, and most people give up because they don't see the ladder. Some of them leap, but they become quickly discouraged because it doesn't come to them instantly. Others keep jumping, knowing that if God sees leaping souls, he will have mercy and will lift them up.

Our task in life, then, is to be leaping souls, even when we are lower than the lowest rung.

Each of us has had at least one of those moments that changed our lives forever. A moment when one action, however simple, made all the difference.

It can be the simplest thing: a phone call or an email from a long-lost friend. It could be something traumatic, like an auto accident. Something that changes the meaning of all that has been and all that will be. Invariably, this incident wakes us from our slumber to a life of service, a life overflowing with meaning, a life of leaping souls and spiritual audacity.

I had one of those moments in April 2008, one of those life-changing moments of clarity that yielded a new level of insight and wisdom and shook me from the numbness of unfathomable pain; when all the climbing and leaping that had seemed for naught yielded a new level of insight and wisdom.

I've often spoken about how hard it is in my profession to juggle the needs of the congregation with the needs of my family. Now that the overwhelming majority of other professionals also consider themselves to be working 24/7, clergy are no longer alone in this, but there remains a big difference in the degree of difficulty. The clergy have many more balls in the air, and each one is a human life. And never was that tested more than that early spring weekend.

Mara and I had to take Ethan down to the emergency room for something that, thank God, didn't turn out to be serious. But at the time we didn't know.

Just as we were about to leave the house, the phone rang. A congregant, a vibrant father of two teenagers, had suddenly collapsed of a brain aneurysm at home and was being rushed unconscious to the very same emergency room.

As Ethan lay on the gurney in his cubicle, waiting for the attending physician, my congregant was just a few cubicles over. His family was also there, facing the most intense scenario imaginable. I was confronted with the ultimate dilemma for a father and a rabbi. I had every excuse to ignore the other family. But I simply couldn't do that. Nor could I give my own child short shrift. For four nightmarish hours, I shuttled from cubicle to cubicle, switching roles from rabbi to dad and back again. I couldn't be there for just one. I had to be present for all. If we had been in the delivery room, it would have been a sitcom. But this took place far from Labor and Delivery.

This was a moment when it would have been easy to snap. The only way to survive such raw terror is to avert its direct gaze. So I switched to autopilot. I had to help everyone else get through while maintaining my own sanity. It would have been easy to bury myself so deep inside my role as to cease feeling anything at all. I walked no easy road; I had no alternative, in fact, but to feel completely and utterly inadequate, incapable of alleviating a pain that cannot be alleviated.

What kind of parent leaves his child in an emergency room to go to work? What kind of rabbi leaves a family in extreme distress in order to attend to personal matters? Never before, not even at my kids' Bar Mitzvahs, had the boundaries between work and family become so blurred, and never before had I faced such a rabbinic *Sophie's Choice*. My choice that night was to be either a horrible parent, a horrible pastor . . . or both.

And I chose both. Because that choice carried within it the only possibility, however slight, of a fourth choice: neither.

I was intrigued to read about how megachurch Pastor Rick Warren juggles so many causes. He said he's an expert time manager. I'm sure Pastor Rick is a good husband and family man in his own way, but something has to give. I felt like I was being an abysmal parent *and* an insufficient rabbi *and* a pretty lousy husband, too. There was no denying it. Pretty bad friend as well.

And think of all the others I've let down! I should have spent four sermons just on that, not to mention what the Chinese are doing to Tibet. I could spend every High Holidays simply hammering home the need to assist Israel. Didn't. Blew it. And what about all the suffering at home, from hurricanes and hunger, homelessness and hopelessness? My congregation includes kids who have nearly died from drinking and were nearly expelled for cheating. What have I done for them? And I've had congregants suffering from horrible illnesses, destructive relationships—people who have lost spouses and parents and children—kids who have lost their first pets. And where have I been?

But then at that moment, in the emergency room, I was redeemed.

I was sitting there with Ethan, still pushing back ruminating on the enormity of my helplessness, and suddenly the curtain swung open. There stood the wife of the congregant who, in the midst of the most chaotic and numbing despair of her life, took a few minutes to lend some comfort to *my* family.

She asked Ethan how *he* was feeling.

I knew then that I was not alone in my predicament. A fellow soul, one who had every right to be even more absorbed in her own pain, was standing alongside me in the trenches.

The wounds are raw. The scars are fresh. The wind is biting cold. But the soul is still leaping! Like moths drawn to a flame, we are drawn to the lights of dawn shining from beyond the top of our ladder—upward and upward. These are the rays of promise and hope.

A little back pain, a slight limp—like Jacob's limp when he fought the angel—a scarred soul, another ring around the trunk. Each of us has experienced a moment that has shaken us to the core, be it profound, like a First Response stick turned blue, a devastating CT scan, or a Dear John email. These are the moments that hit us like a shrill Shofar blast, whose purpose, according to Maimonides, is to rouse us from our slumber. When it happens, my only advice is this:

Take hold of your neighbor's hand, look up to the tops of the mountains from where your help will come, and climb. Feel the wind against your face and the pulse beating in the warm hand you are holding. Feel her pain and your own as best you can, for no one can feel it all, and forgive yourself and others for all the other times. Lovingly embrace the miracle of being alive, and be thankful that even on the bottom rung of Jacob's ladder, down in the deepest trenches of life's emergency room, you are in the company of angels.

Mensch•Mark 14

1990

MY BROTHER'S KEEPER

On Disability and Destiny

My brother, Mark, who is, as we say today, "intellectually challenged," is sixteen months my junior. We shared the same bedroom while growing up, with a partition separating our beds. People often mistook us for twins; I never could see such a resemblance, though I was proud to be identified with him. Our family albums are filled with photos of me holding his hand on roller coasters and kissing him at birthday parties. As a teenager, while most of my friends spent their Friday nights hanging out in someone's basement or at the movies, I often gave Mark a bath.

Life in my home consisted of a bizarre series of recurring vignettes—bizarre to most, normal for me. While my mother bemoaned the fact that we could entertain so rarely, I naively clung to the presumption that our guests would not be fazed by Mark's spontaneous calls of "*kane-meetchee-molin*!!" and "*A-weekee-wee*!!" the occasional flailing of his arms in an unfathomable rage, and his insatiable appetite. Perhaps they would think it cute.

He wasn't toilet trained until late adolescence. Until then, my parents, sister, and I took turns wiping him; not a pleasant task, but one that older siblings of toddlers face every day, I figured. A minor inconvenience. For my parents, Mark's condition was a tragedy; for me, a given.

At night when he was frustrated or just seeking attention, he would bang on the partition until my parents came to check on him. Sometimes, when they delayed, I would just say, "Heck with it," and climb into bed with him until he calmed down. He would play his record player incessantly in our room, repeating the same records over and over again, one of them, somewhat fittingly, Elvis Presley's "Too Much." But I was the perfect middle child. I almost never got mad at him, though one time I accidently closed a car door on his fingers. To this day I'm not sure how accidental it was. But Mark and I were as close as brothers could be. As far as I know, none of my friends got to wipe their brothers' tushes.

I believed the old saying that having a disabled sibling was really a blessing in disguise, a gift that would make me a better person. Therefore, Mark's purpose on earth was to provide me with cheap sensitivity training.

Until we were both in our twenties, I never knew whether his disability resulted from human error or divine decree. The endless search for a definitive cause was for my parents an obsession, for me a curiosity. But in the mid '80s, we finally got the conclusive answer, one that transformed me from observer to survivor.

My brother has fragile X syndrome, a genetic disorder first discovered in 1970 and now recognized as the second leading cause of mental disability among newborns. Fragile X results from a weakness in the genetic structure of the X chromosome. Females, who are born with two Xs, one from each parent, are often less affected by the syndrome because their normal X shields them from the fragile one. Most males born with the defective X are not so lucky.

Genetic screening now can detect fragile X with astounding accuracy. I was tested before I was married. I'm clean. Completely, utterly clean. Not even my great-grandchild could inherit the defect from me. It was a fifty-fifty shot, a flip of the coin. I won.

Of my mother's two X chromosomes, I got the good one.

Mark got the bad one.

If my mother had known then what we know now, she would likely not have had Mark.

Or me.

Mark lives in a group home that my father founded, and spends workdays at a sheltered workshop doing various menial tasks and eagerly awaiting his reward for a job well done: a can of Coke at 1:30. I earn more in a week than he'll earn all year. I vacation in Paris and eat at all the best restaurants. He chows down at the local Burger King. I graduated from an Ivy League college and earned three advanced degrees. With gentle encouragement, Mark can count to twenty. I got married. I drive a car. I have children. I chart my future. He's happy—unbelievably content—with a candy bar and a few old '45s to play on his run-down record player.

In nature's demonic process of selection, Mark was the victim, while I was condemned, in my good fortune, to live out my life knowing it.

Mark has become my mirror image, the X factor defining who I am and what I could easily have become. We are two sides of the same coin. We share the accident of birth.

Mark's rage and frustration live within me. Whenever I forget a meeting or misplace my keys, I grumble heavenward for being hampered with such mundane limitations, sometimes voicing sentiments strikingly similar to the ones Mark used to mutter at the dinner table. And when I see Mark beaming proudly after asking Mom, in a complete and utterly civilized sentence, to pass the chicken "pleeze," my frustration quickly melts into his exultation.

We are Cain and Abel, two halves of a genetic whole, separated before birth. We sleep in separate bedrooms now, 180 miles apart. I wander the face of civilization seeking meaning and imparting my uncertainty to others. Although he wipes himself now, Mark stayed in his garden, shielded from the terrible knowledge I now possess about me, about him, about us all. As my children grow, their fragility exposed, no matter how far I stray, my brother's DNA screams at me from the bowels of the earth.

Mensch•Mark 15

THE PETER PANNING OF AMERICA

Can the Past Remain Ever-Present?

This essay was originally written just at the point when old, dusty home movies were finding a new shelf life in altered formats, enabling childhood to be relived on an endless loop and our inner child to continually reemerge.

Perhaps *the* defining characteristic of the baby boomer is his inexhaustible attachment to his own childhood. Our need to return seems insatiable. Adults rush home from their jobs and flock to films like *Back to the Future* and *Big*, when little boys court their mothers and the aging process is magically reversed.

Just recently I have rediscovered another genre of film that has added a new dimension to my own retrospections: the home movie. Home movies of the '50s and '60s, left in dusty basements for many years, are now gaining a technological resuscitation through the magic of the VCR. I excavated mine, transferred them to videotape, turned on the television, and images that would take a psychiatrist years to draw out of dim memory were suddenly flashing before me like today's news: "Hammerman born; film at 11."

I see a baby being carried from the obstetrics ward, apparently asleep. How small and frail he looks, how barely alive. Minutes pass before I realize that the infant was—is—me. George Santayana wrote, "The fact of having been born is a bad augury for immortality." Now I see why, for I am gazing through the looking glass at a time when my existence was a novelty to my parents and the world.

The next instant reveals my father tossing burgers on the grill; he smiles, unaware that a heart attack will cut short his life at age sixty. I view this bucolic family scene as would Emily in Thornton Wilder's *Our Town*, yearning to return to the fray and rewrite the script. "Don't eat that, Dad! Stay away from the cholesterol! Talk to me! Let's toss the ball. Let's make the most of what time we have left."

I wish to freeze-frame the moment forever, but that is beyond even the capacities of my VCR.

The next moment I see my mother . . . no, my grandmother, also now dead, and she holds me up to the camera. An older version of me stands alongside. Having learned how to decipher the genetic code of this film, I know that the man must be my uncle.

As for the baby—me—I squirm uncomfortably in my grandmother's arms. Funny, in all the photo albums I'm smiling. Movies are far subtler, more frightening than any stills.

My mother appears, as young then as my wife is now. She speaks to the baby. Although I hear none of the dialogue in these silent flicks, it is clear that in her mind I am only a child. Could any legitimate baby boomer not be left wondering how much that relationship has changed?

I see the sacred places of my youth, places to which I thought I'd never return: the snowman on my front lawn, the piano in the living room, the swing set in my backyard. The resurrected people, relatives and friends stare into the camera. And I, the captivated viewer, newly mindful of how precious and fleeting life is, wonder if that is what they are trying to tell me.

No wonder my contemporaries and I obsess about our wonder years, the first generation possessing the power to act on that obsession. We are inexhaustibly attached to childhood precisely because we've never had to leave it. We can go home again, thanks to the unwitting collaboration of amateur and professional filmmakers. In the *Back to the Future* series, Steven Spielberg created the town in which we all could have lived; in *Big*, Tom Hanks masterfully re-created the child we all could have been. And our trusty home movies fill in all the gaps. We can thrill at our own first steps, laugh at our messier feedings, and stare in wonder at our births—as our own children watch alongside.

The home movie and Hollywood film share one inherent weakness: the reel always runs out. Just when the film has resurrected a father's loving glance, filling for an instant an aching vacuum in a grown-up child's soul, the scene shifts cruelly to the Grand Canyon or Disneyland, and we must fast-forward past twenty minutes of Mickey Mouse, only to discover in our fright that Mickey Mouse is where it ends.

The screen goes blank, the child that was fades to black, and we are instantly propelled back to adulthood again. That is, until the next showing.

PART THREE

The Nobility of Normalcy

. . . In which we experience the beauty of a life lived according to the rhythms of sacred time and moral deed. That's been the secret of Judaism's survival for so many centuries of exile; everyday holiness leads to a life of enchantment and purpose, the "Nobility of Normalcy." With modernity came the breakdown of consensus on how a sacred life is to be lived. But it would be tragic to lose it and ennobling to redefine it.

"What day is it?"
"It's today," squeaked Piglet.
"My favorite day," said Pooh.

—A. A. Milne, Winnie-the-Pooh

On the Sabbath, man ceases completely
to be an animal whose main occupation is to fight
for survival and sustain his biological life.
On the Sabbath, man is fully man, with no other
task than that of being human.

—Erich Fromm

Mensch•Mark 16

LIVING ON
THE BACK PAGES

Holiness Lies in the Sacred
Pulse of Daily Life

Boredom is everywhere. It is spreading. And we loathe it. If Americans spent one-tenth of the amount of time searching for a cure for cancer that we do looking for cures for boredom, there would be, quite simply, no more cancer. But spend all the time you want and there still will be no cure for boredom, at least none that money can buy.

It's been suggested that "boredom" comes from the French *bourrir*, meaning "to stuff." As novelist Walker Percy has noted, "Boredom is the self being stuffed with itself." Boredom is the self imprisoned, trapped in a sea of self-help books.

What is known is that the word *boredom* didn't appear at all until the eighteenth century. Does that mean that no one was bored until the 1700s? Or were people bored but too busy in their struggles to survive to notice? It's interesting that we never read of someone from the eighteenth century in search of the perfect sixteenth-century antique chair. The people seemed to be living more in the moment. Boredom appears to be somewhat indigenous to our era of detachment from self.

Boredom can be defined differently by each of us, but objective standards unite our experiences, and they are growing in number.

For all or most of us, boredom is:

- Being forced to sit through an entire collection of miniseries starring Lindsay Wagner.
- Leafing through any magazine found at the checkout counter of the supermarket.
- Standing at the checkout counter of the supermarket.
- Watching C-Span during a filibuster.
- Viewing anyone else's home movies.
- Vacationing at any hotel along an interstate highway that accepts your AAA discount, or
- Spending Saturday night at home, or any other time or place when society informs us that we should be out having fun.

And boredom is the everyday, the routine. Getting up, brushing teeth, showering, dressing, going to the kitchen, eating breakfast, checking the news, starting the car, and by then hopefully saying a few civilized words to the family. Then it's off to your day, office, school, club, dentist, shopping, work, car repair shop. Followed by lunch, back to work, back home, run a few errands, pet the dog, grab dinner, head out for a few meetings, catch the news, or, for a quick summary, the monologue, and then it's off to sleep. Do this for, say, 220 days, and then it's time to dust off that AAA travel guide for a few days of driving and R & R (we're so bored we don't even use full words anymore), settle in at one of those splashy hotels where the most exciting moment is ripping the paper off the seat in the bathroom, the one that says, "Sanitized for your convenience." And we say to ourselves, "That's exactly what we're looking for: sanity. And we've found it."

Am I boring you yet?

If anyone had yelled out an answer to that question, he would be termed in Hebrew a *tardan,* "a heckler." Funny, because the word also means "a bore." The Hebrew word for boredom also means "to drive away, expel." That's exactly what boredom does; it drives us away from real life, from the present moment. It expels the soul. Boredom is the ultimate escape.

In a July 1, 1990, *Newsweek* column entitled "A White-Male Lament," Donald Clement writes of the plight of the BMCWM, the boring, middle-class, white male. BMCWMs don't have causes, he claims, not because they don't care, but because they are "passion impaired." "When you spend eight or ten hours daily getting paid for doing boring things," he writes, "you not only get a lot of practice being boring, you come to prefer being boring because it's so much safer than passion and intensity."

That reminds me of another Hebrew word for boredom: *She'a'moom.* Reverse a couple of the letters and you get the word *Sh'ma,* which means "listen attentively." Attentiveness and wonder are the opposite of boredom. Not fun. Not excitement. Those are just fleeting impulses. Wonder, like boredom, is a state of being. And it's that close, just a matter of a few letters, just a matter of looking at the world only slightly differently.

Judaism celebrates the dull over the dazzling, and in doing so, the dull becomes dazzling. Judaism says, take an ordinary object—a pair of candles, a white cloth, a loaf of bread—and say a few words over them, a blessing, and suddenly the mundane becomes a focus of enchantment. Suddenly the ordinary becomes extraordinary. Suddenly a simple act takes on cosmic significance.

Take two people, say a few words, and you have something holy, a marriage, a family. Take a day and say a few words, drink a sip of wine, and you have a sacred moment in time, an eternal present, the Sabbath. Take an ordinary land, say some words of concern, a pledge to return—say them every day for 2,000 years of wandering, and you have a sacred place, the land of Israel, to which we have returned.

Take a book and fill it with the most boring minutiae imaginable, a book that discusses every detail of life, every act from childbirth to how to put on your shoes in the morning, and you have the Talmud.

There is no boredom in Judaism. There is no routine. Even the routine ceases to be the routine. "The old becomes new and the new becomes holy," in the words of the great Rav Kook. When we look with an inquiring mind at the universe, we're amazed at its beauty and sense of order. We are in awe of a God who had the sense to ensure that species who send their children to college do not typically have litters of six or more.

I say it's time for us to dare to be dull.

The Dull Men's Club, a loosely organized forum that proposes to speak for millions of Americans—the ones not listed in "Who's Who," who have never joined a fitness club and wear pajamas to bed. Their former president, Joseph Troise, says that America's strength comes from its dull people. "Behind every flashy façade sits a humorless and fastidiously competent drone who keeps the whole ship afloat."

They established a Museum of the Ordinary in Carroll, Iowa, a run-down building on the edge of town, which includes a collection of ashtrays from all fifty states, a collection of hubcaps, and an exhibit of bowling balls. The organization has no budget and no convention, and Mr. Troise has never tasted Perrier. They have also proposed such adventures as a bus tour of New Jersey golf courses. "Let's face it," he says. "A lot of people are under pressure to be interesting, to be trendy. But it's a no-win situation. Sooner or later, you're going to meet someone who has a more expensive Porsche or a larger hot tub."

And we should somehow try to appreciate the wonders of the ordinary, to look beyond the headlines of the news, because on the back pages of the newspaper is where real life is lived. These stories, of weddings and births and small deeds of unknown heroes, are the main headlines of the eternal human struggle. As we adjust our perspective and look beneath the surface of time, we discover that people haven't changed that much at all, and that continuity is reassuring. History happens on page one, but real life takes place in the back.

Following are some clips from the back pages of the *Stamford Advocate*, the local rag. While the articles might seem boring and insignificant by our standards, it is those very standards that we need to overcome. Let's dare to be dull and take a look.

> A parking ticket, placed on an automobile Saturday by policeman Thomas Hogan, cost Andrew Wasco, 22, of Lockwood Ave, $3.40. Wasco protested the ticket and flipped a lighted cigarette at the policeman to give vent to his feelings and was subsequently fined $5 for breach of peace.

People, like nations, get angry. Like nations, people have their limits; they won't be abused by the system. Sometimes, enough is simply enough. The date? *December 7, 1941*, a date that, for Mr. Hogan, surely lived in infamy.

> Mr. and Mrs. Murray Zwart of Glenbrook announce the birth of their first son, Curtis Dale Zwart, at Stamford Hospital. Mrs. Zwart is the former Miss Phyllis Gallup, daughter of Mr. and Mrs. A. Judson Gallup of Glenbrook.

Congratulations to the Zwarts and to Curtis Dale, who was, by the way, not the only one to be born on *May 14, 1948*.

It seems a waste to let geranium plants freeze to death in the late fall and then have to buy new ones each spring to give your garden the beautiful touch that these flowers provide. You may prevent complete waste by trying to keep the old plants alive indoors through the winter. Or you may take cuttings and root them to get a head start on spring, if you have the adequate space and growing conditions.

This gardening tip teaches a profound lesson about maintaining hope for life in the face of nature's annual drama of death and tragedy known as fall. A lesson for any autumn, including that one. The date: *November 22, 1963.*

Dear Ann Landers: Please tell men not to marry because they feel sorry for the girl and figure on making her over into something better after marriage. It never works. Both my husband and my son made this mistake. After they grew weary of their "inferior" wives, they found younger women who were more attractive and more interesting. The heartache is unbearable. My daughter-in-law turns to me for comfort, never suspecting that for me it is the second time.—History repeats itself.

This day, the day when history repeated itself, was *July 20, 1969.* This is a day when one desperate woman took one small step toward inner peace by reaching out to Ann Landers for help. And in embracing her daughter-in-law in her time of need, thereby dispelling all those mother-in-law stereotypes, she took one giant leap for womankind.

In observance of Brotherhood Month, Dr. Russell McGown, pastor of the First Congregational Church, and Rabbi David Pearlman of Temple Beth El will exchange pulpits this week. Dr. McGown will preach at the 8:30 PM service at the temple, Friday, and Rabbi Pearlman will speak at the 11:00 AM service at the

Congregational Church on Sunday. On Saturday, the services will be conducted by the post Bar Mitzvah group, led by Howard Kahner and Arthur Selkowitz.

The story appeared in the issue of *February 14, 1957*, a date of enormous historical importance.

For me, at least. It was the day I was born.

It is behind the front pages where we read about life as it really happens. The front page is interesting and important, but it's the dull bits of social chatter, the gardening tips, birth announcements, and police blotters, the boring, the dull, the everyday. This is the wondrous world we inhabit.

This wondrous life. Every day of it, every moment.

Waking up is special. A new day. A second chance. Resurrection with the sun. Throw off the blankets and listen to the rooster . . . I mean alarm clock. Neither one remembers yesterday.

Stretching, brushing teeth, rediscovering the miracle of complexity known as the human body, washing, dressing, opening our eyes to a new day. Our tradition has blessings for each of these actions. Even without a prayer book handy, simply by appreciating these everyday miracles, you are praying.

And meals are special. A good cup of coffee. A trip to the grocery store, a friendly hello to all those other human complexities on the street. A reciprocated smile from everyone in the office. And then a new challenge at your desk. A phone call to make, a project to complete. Carpooling to dance class or, better yet, to Hebrew school with three laughing shrieking little fifth grade complexities in the backseat. A miracle.

And then the hero's return. At day's end, like Ulysses or King David, the warrior comes home, having triumphed or having failed, for now, but having fought and having lived to fight another day.

And we sit down, and we take our piece of bread in hand, and we enjoy it; every morsel—and every moment of this precious gift that we have been given, these years of life.

God knows how long our lives will be. But unless we see the miracle of it every day, not one of those years is worth a thing.

The past and future, those are the domain of the bored. Our concern is where they intersect. Here and now. We must grab on to this present and hug it until it begs for mercy.

We have the chance to become heroes, legendary figures in the Book of Life. Armed with a toothbrush instead of a sword, we celebrate the victory of the routine, the dull and the everyday; the evisceration of apathy.

And there is nothing boring about that.

Mensch•Mark 17

1998

THE FORBIDDEN OREO

We Are What We Eat

This Mensch•Mark *explores a key area of everyday holiness, the dietary laws, but with a new twist: the twist of an Oreo cookie. The Oreo's becoming kosher came to be seen as a watershed event for American Jewry, partly because of this essay, which was originally published in* The New York Times Magazine.

The news came racing across the internet with apocalyptic urgency. My rabbinical chat group was abuzz with incredible tidings. Could it finally be true? No, we don't have a Jewish president yet, but something almost equally astounding has transpired, a telltale sign that Jews have finally made it. After eighty-five years in the gentile larder, Oreos have gone kosher.

With the possible exception of Santa Claus and the Big Mac, the self-proclaimed "King of Cookies" has long been the most infamous forbidden fruit from which observant Jewish children have kept their distance. As our mouths watered at the mere mention of this unsupervised delicacy, we assuaged our deprived taste buds with inferior sawdust- textured hybrids and swallowed our yearning for Oreo mix-ins at the ice cream parlor. Some kids dreamed of catching a Mickey Mantle foul pop; I fantasized about unscrewing an Oreo and licking the middle.

I called Nabisco to confirm the good news, and it got even better. Not only are Oreos now kosher, but so are Ritz Bits, Honeymaid Grahams, and many other products. In truth, these edibles could have passed muster a decade ago when an increasingly health-conscious Nabisco began replacing animal fat with vegetable shortening in its products.

I should be thrilled at this news. If the cookie moguls are finding it cost-effective to answer to a higher authority, that's because more people are opting to bring God into the kitchen. And it's not just Jews. Kosher food is increasingly popular among Muslims (who have similar dietary laws), vegetarians, and undoubtedly many who wonder how U.S. government inspectors could have let so many tainted burgers make it to the freezers of Burger King last summer.

Domestic sales of products targeted to the kosher consumer now exceed $3 billion annually, having achieved double-digit increases for each of the past five years. The Orthodox Union alone claims 250,000 products under its supervision.

Eating these days is an act of faith . . . and fear. We can't understand most of what is on the label, but when we see a kosher symbol, many naively assume that a pious old religious guy personally inspects and gives God's blessing to each item. While that myth is overblown and kosher products might not always be healthier, Jewish dietary laws promote the type of self-control that often leads to healthier living. They are based on a value system that sanctifies life, limits the pain of animals, and views the body as a temple; all of which places these ancient principles in confluence with the current zeitgeist and has made the kosher symbol into this generation's Good Housekeeping seal.

But now that kosher is "in" and Oreos are permissible, I'm not sure I want them to be. Not that I want my children to suffer, but I know that in some perverse manner my Oreo envy kept me safely at the outer edges of Middle America, shielding me from total absorption into the vanilla masses.

More than anything else, the Jewish contribution to American culture has been through communicating the experience of marginality, of having survived Otherness. Oreo denial was, for me, a direct extension of Egyptian slavery; it made me uncomfortable enough to feel different and different enough to feel proud.

Even those Jews who always ate Oreos will now lose out. They have one less whopper of a sin to notch to their defiant belts ("Take that, Rabbi Marcus! And furthermore, we served 'em with shrimp at Joey's Bar Mitzvah!"). The news leaves us utterly confused, much as Adam and Eve would have felt had God suddenly appeared to them years later, saying, "You know that fruit, the one that caused all the trouble? Well, it's okay now. Here, unscrew it. Take a lick." Which taboo will be the next to fall? Bestiality? Murder? The Hostess Twinkie?

I can recall my first Twinkie. I was around eight. She was blonde, soft and spongy, sweet and sensational. It just felt right. Mamie, my matronly Irish babysitter, knew little of the tribal taboos imposed on my home. Sure, she kept her ham sandwiches to herself and never fed me milk with meat. But how was she to know that this innocent snack was as verboten as a slab of bacon? It was just a Twinkie, and she offered it to me. So what was I to do? I was hooked. For weeks on end, Mamie supplied me with Twinkies. Eventually, both Mamie and the Twinkies disappeared. She never had the chance to get me on to Oreos.

It is almost midnight. I'm sitting at my kitchen table, sampling my first batch of the previously prohibited cookie. Holding it up to the light, I scrutinize this marvelous black medallion with the embossed OREO surrounded by a wreath of posies. I feel so normal. So American. I shudder. Has the Jewish condition ever been compatible with normalcy? Can we survive this?

A more formidable dilemma lies before me: to dunk, bite, or unscrew? As I hum, "A kid'll eat the middle of an Oreo first . . ." I begin to twist the top carefully with my left hand, holding the bottom cookie steady with my right.

The top breaks in half.

I eat the broken cookie. It's good, but I crave a Twinkie. The thrill is gone.

The Oreo, enduring symbol of hollowness for African Americans, reveals the masks Jews wear as well. As noble distinctions continue to crumble and cherished customs gain universal appeal, I am beginning to understand that a faith community cannot live by food taboos alone. True, we are what we eat, but we must be more.

Mensch•Mark 18

THE INVISIBLE FENCE

Setting Behavioral Boundaries

Living a life of everyday holiness involves a tremendous amount of discipline and boundary setting. I learned about that from my dog Crosby, who died at the age of fifteen in 2017 but remained loving and loyal, right up until the end. I dedicate this to him, to his younger sister, Chloe, to Cassidy and Casey, who have taken his place in the Hammerman poodle pantheon, and to his predecessor, Maggie, a feisty black lab who really could have used an Invisible Fence.

My dog Crosby is a cute, black standard poodle who loves everything that moves. So when we brought him home, Mara and I worried that he might come to love the cars whizzing by on the road in front of our house a little too much. We decided to install what is called an "Invisible Fence."

It's a lovely name. I guess the people in marketing decided against calling it the Electro-Shock Dog Zapper or Stalag Fido.

Training Crosby with the special collar was not easy. We all have those "this will hurt me more than it hurts you" moments with our loved ones, but I'm reasonably sure it hurt him more than it hurt me. The jolt might have been invisible, but Crosby's yelps told me that it was very real. And within a few sessions, Crosby was trained.

The irony is that now that he has been restricted to the area within the fence, Crosby has been liberated, and he's happier than ever. He can run free all over the yard, while before he had to be on the leash. And while he might occasionally look forlornly at the green grass on the other side of that invisible barrier, he leaps and barks far, far away from the dangers of Roxbury Road. Even if he were to shed the special collar, he would still stay behind the Invisible Fence. One might call it force of habit, or one could call it structure and security.

There was that one time he was so excited to see my neighbor's young daughters that he leaped across the line. So there was Crosby, suddenly on the other side of the fence, off leash, free to do whatever he wanted. He could have run to Manhattan if he wanted, or joined the circus, or hopped a flight to Paris where the poodles run the show.

But he froze, for just a second, in discombobulated disbelief. Mr. Liberated-High-and-Mighty Poodle was not so happy after all.

It's not just dogs, of course, who prosper from living within limits. Robert Frost is not the only one to understand that good fences make good neighbors.

Good fences make good neighbors—and no fences make for chaos. In 2003, Crosby wasn't the only Hammerman to feel the tug of an invisible fence. For the first time, both Daniel and Ethan were at overnight camp for an extended period of several weeks. When we dropped them off, Mara and I looked at each other and realized that we didn't have to go home! There was something very disconcerting about the sudden freedom we had, about not having to worry about getting a babysitter, about being able to go out for dinner without having to make elaborate preparations weeks ahead of time.

When I left home for college, I looked forward to relaxing some of the ritual practices I had grown up with. It was my freshman ten. I shed ten *mitzvahs* (Jewish obligations). But I soon found myself missing the intimacy of being with family and community on Shabbat. The restrictions that had been imposed on me in my youth became my chosen anchor during those turbulent college years. My observance level was still more relaxed than it had been, but the rhythm of my week still revolved around Shabbat dinners at Hillel.

People react strangely to sudden liberation. When the ancient Israelites were freed from Egypt, the first thing they did was loot and pillage. I read about an Egyptian, Dr. Nabil Hilmi, who filed a lawsuit against "all the Jews of the world" for recovery of property allegedly stolen during the Exodus. According to Dr. Hilmi's mathematical computations, which include an annual doubling in value of the material in question, 1,125 trillion tons of gold are owed by the Jews for each of the 300 tons he estimates was taken. And that doesn't include interest, which he claims, without explanation, should be calculated for 5,758 years.

Dr. Hilmi knows his Bible, but evidently he does not know his Talmud. The Talmud tells of precisely such a claim lodged over 2,000 years ago in a world court of sorts presided over by none other than Alexander the Great. A man named Geviha ben Pesisa responded on the Jews' behalf, addressing those very same accusations by asking for compensation for all the man-hours labored by 600,000 Jews during the 430 years of Egyptian slavery. The Egyptians, the Talmud continues, then asked Alexander for three days during which to formulate a response. He granted the recess, but the representatives, finding no counter-argument, never returned.

The Jews owe the Egyptians nothing, but neither does that justify the looting that took place at that time.

The exact same thing happened when Saddam Hussein was overthrown in Iraq. Trying to impose order was impossible once that genie had been let loose from the bottle. So at the same time Saddam's statue came down, we were seeing scenes of massive looting on such a grand scale as to be almost comical, except that it was tragic. Looters took everything but the kitchen sink. Then I tuned in the news one evening and saw an Iraqi walking down the street carrying in his arms a kitchen sink. This is what happens when you suddenly take away the invisible fence.

Now don't get me wrong. I'm not a big fan of dictatorships. Slavery is not a good thing. But fences can be.

So I was looking for an anniversary card down at the Hallmark store and came across this beaut:

To My Wife
Even after all this time in captivity
I love you.

I did not buy it.

Yes, people complain about marriage, using expressions like "the old ball and chain." People complain all the time—except me. I'm totally happy. But we need that invisible fence.

Monogamous marriage trains humans, much like Crosby being zapped trained him. Maybe some of the same technology can be employed. I can just see it now: "Marriage Zapper: Simply slip this collar around your spouse's neck and let him roam freely."

I believe that monogamy was one of the best things ever invented. It teaches us self-discipline. We learn loyalty. We learn not always to be grabbing for more but to be satisfied with what we have. Just as with the Invisible Fence, it teaches us not to mess up someone else's backyard.

Yet I was fascinated to discover that monogamous societies are the exception rather than the rule. Among mammals, only about 5 percent of species practice it. And among human societies, according to *Murdoch's Ethnographic Atlas*, over 72 percent permit multi-spousal relationships. Judaism didn't climb off this bandwagon until Rabbi Gershom banned polygamy in the tenth century, and some non-Western Jews continued the practice until the twentieth century. But monogamy was already predominant in many Jewish communities much earlier, and Talmudic law set firm boundaries on marriage especially to protect women.

Judaism calls marriage the ultimate act of holiness—*Kiddushin*—and that is symbolized by the drawing of boundaries; the circling that is often done under the wedding canopy is really the marking of a holy boundary, enclosing and protecting the couple within that sacred space. It seems clear, though, that left on our own, without that invisible fence symbolized by the wedding ring, human beings would be much more naturally inclined to swap spouses like so many baseball cards.

You know, this invisible fence idea was invented by Jews. There is something called an *Eruv*, that somewhat physical but primarily metaphysical boundary within which traditional Jews can carry on Shabbat. The Talmud also instructs us to build a "fence around the Torah." The idea was that we should consciously avoid behaviors that might place us in a position where we could violate a law of the Torah. Traditionally, this principle has been cited as a justification for everything from the lighting of Shabbat candles eighteen minutes before sunset to the prohibition of legumes on Passover (by Jews of European ancestry) to the separation of milk and meat. The Torah says nothing about two sets of dishes. It just says we can't cook a goat in its mother's milk. The rabbis instituted the separation of milk and meat, pots and pans so that there would be no possibility that anyone, even accidentally, would boil a kid in the milk of its own mother. The Torah doesn't say chicken is meat, by the way. But God forbid you should mistake a chicken cutlet for a veal cutlet and mistakenly boil the veal in its mother's milk, so the rabbis placed chicken in the meat category for just that reason. That's how a "fence around the Torah" works. It often seems arbitrary, and in some cases Jews have gone much too far, but the principle is sound.

The rabbis had little trust in human nature. They had good reason. They lived in a time where people had little self-control. Not much has changed.

Today, Crosby is a very happy dog, except that he now has a sister, Chloe, who bosses him like crazy. He has his fence; he has his crate; he loves them both, but he is nobody's slave.

Mensch•Mark 19

THE POWER GRID

Recognizing the Limits and Potential of One's Power

In August 2003, my family took that great journey Americans have undertaken since the days of Lewis and Clark. We went to the national parks out West. Then for a change of pace, we spent a couple of days in Las Vegas, following in the pioneering footsteps of Lewis and Martin.

During those two weeks, we experienced immeasurable expressions of divine power and countless wonders, enough to make you shake with trepidation and bend the knee with awe. I carried around cards containing many Hebrew blessings to be recited upon seeing amazing natural phenomena, and my challenge to my kids before the vacation was to see if we could have the chance to recite every blessing of wonder found on the card before the trip was done. They told me to "chill" (we *had* to take this trip with a rabbi?) but then joined me in the quest.

The first stop is Yellowstone and we find ourselves standing in a living, bubbling caldera. The earth is literally breathing, it is spitting up water, it is gurgling, it is making the most godawful gaseous smells—like a baby. The land, quite literally, is coming alive.

All around me is devastation, the most beautiful devastation I've ever seen: miles and miles of ashen, burned-out trees destroyed by the wildfires of 1988; fires that became catastrophic because generations of our hubris prevented nature from taking its course. In the brush are young trees, sprouting amid the devastation, fragrant and pure. I recite the blessing on fragrant trees, *boray atzei besamim*, "Blessed are you, Lord our God, who creates fragrant trees."

I stand by Yellowstone Lake looking out on Saturday night as wildfires rage over the east entrance to the park. Two intermingled bursts of flame lighting the distant sky with God's power look like some heavenly Havdalah candle, the large candle with intertwined wicks and an enormous flame, which is lit as part of the ceremony ending the Sabbath. I hum the Havdalah melody as the smoke hovers overhead.

We see lots of glorious creatures in Yellowstone, bald eagles and falcons, and herds of bison all across the hillsides. We actually see a place where the deer and the antelope play. So I recite the blessing for extraordinary creatures.

We drive through the Grand Tetons, where snowcapped mountains pierce the sky, good for another blessing. The first one, *oseh ma'ase breisheet*, "Who makes the works of creation." Mountains have the power to awaken an overwhelming sense of the sacred. We stop in Jackson Hole, where they thank God daily for designer cowboy boots.

A few days later we are on our way to Zion National Park, driving through southern Utah into some mountains where the clouds are ominous and thick, and the lightning perilously close. The rain clouds engulf the mountains out West, something I'm not used to seeing in Connecticut, though I've seen it in Jerusalem many times. And with the wind kicking up something awful, we stop at a Dairy Queen along the interstate and ask the cashier if there are tornadoes in these parts. She says yes, but don't worry, they are usually not too bad. At this point I'm ready to pick up Toto and run for cover. We make it through the storm, but we later find out that the same storm flooded Las Vegas, turning The Venetian into Venice. Coincidently, when we left Yellowstone, we had just missed an earthquake.

I'm feeling very lucky but keenly aware of my own smallness. Daily I am witnessing earthquakes, floods, wildfires, and the most gorgeous sunrises and sunsets I've ever seen. To be standing at Bryce Canyon with these human-looking rock formations, which the Native Americans call "legend people" (hoodoos), who were turned to stone because of their sins, is to be reminded of how sin can turn human hearts to stone. And to be in at the canyon floor of Zion National Park or at the rim of the Grand Canyon is to know what it must have been like to be at the shores of the Red Sea.

What's totally natural appears supernatural, perfection and balance painted on an enormous canvas. As the author Linda Hogan wrote, "The cure for soul sickness is not in books. It is written in the bark of a tree, in the moonlit silence of night, in the bank of a river and the water's motion. The cure is outside ourselves."

By the time we reached the Grand Canyon, we had been able to recite nearly every blessing on the card, including that all-important one for going to the bathroom. We even drove through some hail, which has a different blessing not on the card, and we saw Mars closer to earth than ever before. We'd experienced every blessing except the one for a rainbow. All we needed was the rainbow.

Looking over the South Rim, I could see a beautiful sunset, and right next to it, a thunderstorm. There had to be a rainbow, somewhere. And sure enough, Mara noticed it first, over to the right, miles and miles from the thundercloud, there it was. It was about seven on a Friday evening. We recited the final blessing, and the Sabbath began. Now I could put the blessing card down and God could rest. But the miracles never stop, and they never fail to shock and awe.

Back on the first day of the trip, just after I watched Old Faithful burst out with steam shooting up into the sky, I tried to call home for messages, but my machine didn't pick up. Only later did I find out why. While I was in the midst of experiencing the greatest power display on earth, the entire East Coast had been thrown into darkness. Fifty million people stood helpless in the August heat back in 2003, victims not of divine power but of a terrible man-made hubris.

Where were you when the lights went out? I was at Old Faithful, where there were no subways, no high-rise elevators, no TV. I was at Yellowstone, where the sky was being lit up by the stars and the forests illumined by a thousand degrees of conflagration. And I felt vulnerable but empowered, knowing that a power far greater than I has bathed me in enormous responsibility.

Where were you when the lights went out? Were you in the subway? In an elevator? In the kitchen with suddenly nothing to cook but a lifetime to thaw? Were you sweating, exposed to the elements with no A/C? Were you at the airport, grounded? Or stuck in the air? Were you in a hospital, at the mercy of tightly rationed auxiliary generators? Did you feel vulnerable? Did you fear terrorism? Did you understand, did you finally understand, just how limited we are? The power grid is a perfect symbol of our hubris, of our presumed power, and of how instantly it all can come tumbling down.

Yes, in 2003 Americans were humbled by the limits of our authority. The world's greatest superpower had failed to defeat small guerrilla armies of terrorists despite its military capability to shock and awe. We had touched the moon and seen through Hubble's eyes the farthest reaches of the universe, but we lacked the wherewithal to check the underside of Columbia's wing before reentry. We had developed the ability to create artificial life, but we couldn't save a set of adult conjoined twins. We had seen loved ones suffer and die, we'd seen the rich and famous succumb to these same diseases as well, and we were powerless to prevent it. Again and again we were reminded of our limits.

Power and its limitations are a prime concern of a central prayer of the daily liturgy, known as the *Alenu*. This magnificent prayer speaks of a future time when all humanity will be united under a single standard of morality and goodness, enhancing the prospects of harmony and peace. It doesn't promise that we'll get there soon but asserts that it is our responsibility to make progress toward that end. That's what the word *Alenu* means: "it is up to us." But that responsibility is a long-term, multigenerational contract requiring patience and persistence.

And the prayer gives us enormous license to exercise that power. We too often speed through the second paragraph of the *Alenu*, but there we see a prime goal of Judaism as being "*l'taken olam bmalchut shaddai*," "to repair the world, to perfect the world, under divine sovereignty." It is from this passage that we get the expression for world repair, *tikkun olam*, that has become increasingly popular among activists of all stripes.

We have been given incredible power to do good, as long as we recall that the ultimate source of our power comes from somewhere else.

A Hasidic master once said that every person should carry two pieces of paper, one in your right-hand pocket and the other in your left. On one of the pieces, you write the verse "For my sake the world was created." On the other piece, you write a very different verse, "I am but dust and ashes."

We are so powerful and yet so humbled.

And that is why, even as we exercise enormous power, we need to pray.

How I wish I were back at Yellowstone right now, bathed in the mist of the geyser, warmed by the glow of a hundred-acre inferno a couple of miles away. Things were a lot less complicated there, where the deer and the antelope play, cradled in the womb of God. How terrifying it is to have the world on our shoulders. I feel the weight of the burden.

But I'm a big boy now. We're all big boys and girls. And God has given us the keys to the Hummer. God has given us the intelligence to split the atom and recork a wine bottle. God has given us the power to topple dictators and build towers that reach beyond the clouds.

We pray for guidance that we can forge a better world for our children. And we give thanks. For it is good to give thanks unto the Lord. For God's power is everywhere to be found. In each mountain, each lovely creature, and each rainbow. And it is the power of kindness, the power of love.

Mensch•Mark 20

PARADISE IN A SANDBOX

Recovering the Pure Faith of a Child

Deuteronomy proclaims that the Torah "is not in the heavens." On the contrary, as I learned early in my career, everyday holiness is as earthbound as the nearest box of sand. In these untethered times, the sandbox is where a sense of order can begin to challenge the new norms of political incivility. When I ask little Celia to speak in complete sentences, or to use her indoor voice, or not to accuse the synagogue next door of sending us their rapists and murderers, I feel downright insubordinate and out of step with the Trump era. It's time to return to our roots.

It is said by some skeptics that too many baby boomers brought up their children to be "snowflakes," each one unique and special, worthy of participation trophies even when they've lost the race. But the Talmud teaches that all humans are, in fact, unique; each is special in his or her own way and that each human life is of equal value before God. And,

as we've seen from the activism of teens in our day, snowflakes have a
tendency to band together and become snowballs, rolling downhill with
a zealous ferocity that sends those same skeptics scurrying into their
woodsheds for a shovel.

The sandbox is where moral resistance begins.

You've probably heard of Robert Fulghum's bestselling collection of essays *All I Really Need to Know I Learned in Kindergarten.* Well, with my most sincere apologies to the author, I must say that all I really needed to know about *religion* I also learned in kindergarten. If only I'd realized this before Mr. Fulghum came along, I might have saved myself five long years in rabbinical school and gone directly from the sandbox to the pulpit.

So what were those precious, irreplaceable lessons of kindergarten?

How to Pray

Among my first prayers was the children's song "If You're Happy and You Know It" (clap your hands). It is most difficult for the adult to replicate the purity and joy of that simple prayer to a deeply perceived yet unarticulated God. Now, if I'm happy I usually don't know it, and if I know it, I don't show it. Like most adults, I tend to do most of my praying when I'm unhappy. And, like most adults, I need a prayer book to pray. When I'm holding a prayer book, it's all but impossible to clap my hands.

How to See God in a Dancing Snowflake

And how to run outside and join that snowflake in its whirling dance. Like a blowing snowflake, a child can dance without ever touching the ground. Few adults this side of Peter Pan and Michael Jordan know what it feels like to fly—and to believe. As Rabbi Lawrence Kushner wrote, "There are places children go that grown-ups can only observe from afar."

How to Love My Neighbor as Myself

"And my neighbor's frog, his kitten, his teddy bear, even his G.I. Joe, everything of my neighbor's, in fact, and everything of my own, too," says the kindergarten student. "Except for my baby brother."

Thou Shalt Not Covet

Because, if thou art a young child, thou knowest not yet how to count. As soon as those cometh to realize that "this little piggy" that runs *wee, wee, wee* all the way home happens to be the *fifth* little piggy, and thou starteth to ask thyself whether everyone has five of these porcine appendages on each foot, and whether thy piggies are bigger than thy neighbor's piggies, that's where the trouble begins.

We Can Live Forever

If, as experts tell us, children cannot truly fathom their mortality until around the age of ten, a preschooler would have no need of an afterlife. For him, this life is eternal life, heaven on earth, paradise in a sandbox. For us, the challenge is to live with the same verve, confidence, and commitment, given our great handicap, the excruciating understanding that our sandbox is actually an hourglass.

One wonders just how certain key historical figures were treated when they were in kindergarten. Was Napoleon habitually ousted from his sandbox? What on earth did Arnold Palmer do in his? Was Karl Marx forced to clean the erasers daily by a slave-driving teacher? Did Freud walk in on an unscheduled tryst in the faculty lounge?

In kindergarten, I learned to trust and respect other human beings. As a young rabbi-to-be, I also learned to respect their differing traditions. If Johnny chose to drink his milk *before* eating his Ring Ding, I couldn't understand it but respected him for it.

No wonder children play such a central role in most religious traditions. In the Seder, the reenactment of Passover drama that takes place annually in Jewish homes, the youngest child asks the Four Questions, thereby setting into motion the entire ritual. Without the child, or some adult representing one, there is no Seder.

Ostensibly, the purpose of the Seder is to transmit an ancient story to the next generation. In truth, however, it is the children who have much to teach their parents; for they already know everything we ever wanted to know about religion . . . but were afraid to ask.

PART FOUR

Pain and Perseverance

. . . In which I deal with personal affliction and the larger tableau of collective calamity. The human rabbi must first learn how to navigate passage through the valley of the shadow to then discover how to transcend it. As Rabbi Levi Yitzchak of Berdichev said over two centuries ago, "It is not why I suffer that I wish to know, but only whether I suffer for Your sake." And that which makes us most human is our ability to persevere. Or as Mark Twain quipped, "Pain is universal. Suffering is optional."

"I don't feel very much like Pooh today," said Pooh. "There there," said Piglet. "I'll bring you tea and honey until you do."

—A. A. Milne, Winnie-the-Pooh

Mensch•Mark 21

THE OTHER SIDE OF THE BED

Healer as Patient

In journalism school I had a chance to spend a day at Riker's Island prison. It was important for a reporter to understand what it feels like to be behind bars. Similarly, every pastor should spend a night in the hospital. In 2011, I got to spend three—during a hurricane.

On a Friday evening in late August of 2011, as I was leading services, I began to experience discomfort in my abdomen that, by the time I got home, had become severe pain. When it got to the point where I could neither lie down, sit, nor stand, I realized I had few choices left. I went to the emergency room where, after a couple of agonizing hours, the problem was diagnosed as a kidney stone. I spent the next three nights in the hospital, right through a hurricane. For the next few weeks, that stone—or, more precisely, the *pain* caused by that stone—became the defining factor of my life.

When I was in the hospital, they kept asking me, on a scale of one to ten, how much pain I was feeling. I was never sure what to answer. If I said a ten, I'd come off as a wimp. There are people who endure much more pain than this. I know. I have, too. I've been to the dentist! Football players feel more pain than this while they're still singing the national anthem. But if I said "two," where would that get me? They'd wonder why I'd even bothered to come. I hovered at somewhere around a six and a half, but I really just wanted to say, "A lot." I'm not sure pain can be quantified. The only way I can describe it to you is to say that the morphine didn't help. I'm not sure you can ever say that my pain is greater than your pain, or the pain of a kidney stone is greater than the pain of a broken leg, or the breakup of a marriage or a sudden death in the family. It's all pain. It all hurts. For me, in fact, the proper number at that moment was infinity. All that mattered was the pain. Everything else became secondary.

Until this experience, I'd never had to stay overnight in the hospital for an illness of my own. I had visited Stamford Hospital literally more than a thousand times over the prior two and a half decades, but until that moment I had always been on the caregiver side of the bed. This experience was very different. It will help me, for sure, to be a better pastor, but an in-service training class would have been fine, thank you very much.

It hit home, just how different this was, when the priest came by and he blessed me. And we know each other well. But when Father Peter Dora came in, this was different. I was the patient.

I felt defrocked in his eyes and my own. But I appreciated being in his prayers.

I now realize just how helpless a patient feels. The nursing staff were terrific, and I have a new appreciation for the work they do.

They were angels responding to every prayer, and most of the prayers involved pain management. But I was totally dependent on them. Every movement was difficult. With the IV in me, my mobility was severely limited and showering was out of the question. And even the slightest twist of the IV tube would result in that annoying beep and I'd have to call the nurse to reset it.

With Hurricane Irene coming, I thought, "At least I'm in the one building in town guaranteed not to lose power." But you might recall that Irene was the Northeast's sneak preview for Sandy, a global warning that global warming was about to kick into high gear. For the first time ever, New York's subway system shut down due to a natural disaster, and along the East Coast nearly 9 million homes and businesses lost power.

At 5:00 AM on Sunday, the hospital lost power. The emergency generator kicked in to maintain essential services, but evidently hot and cold food are not considered essential. And with the A/C off, it became uncomfortably steamy. The only thing air conditioned in the whole room was the back of my gown.

With no TV, I lost touch with much of the outside world. The shades were closed and windows shut tight, so I could barely notice the howling winds of Irene. I lost all sense of time, except in counting the hours between medications. Given the weather and subsequent state of emergency, no one could visit, which I was okay with, because I felt lousy and looked even worse. It also kept me from reenacting that classic scene in which the synagogue president visits the rabbi in the hospital and gives him the good news that the board had passed a resolution calling for his full recovery, by a vote of eight to five.

I tried to sleep, assisted by the pain medication. The room kept getting darker and darker, and I felt myself closing more and more, cocoon-like, into myself. I found myself wanting to be alone yet feeling lonely at the same time.

I wondered if that's how everyone feels, and whether it really helps when I come by to visit patients, with my prime role being to reconnect them to the outside world, to reengage them, to unite them with something beyond their own pain. Can anything I do really make that pain go away? And I wondered whether those patients who are asleep when I come to visit are really asleep, or if they just don't want to deal with visitors.

I wondered, "Had *I* visited me, would I have appreciated it, or would I have pretended to be asleep?"

By the third day, the day after the storm, I was attuned almost exclusively to the rhythms of my own pain. The world around me simply did not exist. The same nursing staff cycled back a few times, so I got to know them. But interestingly, not one asked what I do. It's just one of the ways that the pain transports you to a totally different world. When you're in *here*, it doesn't matter what you do *out there*. In fact, I didn't want a fuss made over me. I asked once about whether they had kosher vegetarian food and got a "say *what?*" look that made me realize this wasn't the check-in counter at La Guardia.

During the afternoons, my fever would spike as the pain returned. In a moment of weakness, I remarked to the nurse, "This is a nightmare." She looked somewhat taken aback. And then I heard a voice within me. This is the only time that voice came out. It was the voice of the guy who has been on the other side of that bed at least once a week for the prior twenty-five years:

Idiot! Are you kidding me? This is a nightmare? Walk down the hall and I'll show you a real nightmare. Walk down the hall and visit the people who don't know if they will ever get that inane wristband removed until it's replaced by a toe tag.

You call yourself unlucky? You're *walk*ing out of here.

You feel pain, but you're walking out of here. People are dying in here and you're carrying on and kvetching because of a little pebble. Get a grip!

Man up!

After that, I was okay. Grubby, but okay. I realized my pain might feel infinite, but it is also relative. And I recalled a story.

A farmer was riding into town on horse and buggy with a load of grain, when he was struck by a car. Seriously injured in the accident, the farmer filed a claim, but his insurance company didn't want to pay, so he was dragged into court. The lawyer representing the insurance company asked him: "Sir, while you were lying at the scene of the accident, is it not true that when asked how you were feeling, you answered: 'I never felt better'?"

"Yes," the farmer answered, "that is true."

"I have no further questions," the lawyer said.

The farmer's lawyer, on redirect, asked his client: "Can you tell me the circumstances in which you said, 'I never felt better'?"

"Sure," the farmer said. "After the accident, I was lying on the ground and the deputy sheriff walked over to my horse, saw that its legs were broken, took out his revolver, and put him out of his misery. He then looked at my dog, also very badly hurt and in great pain, and did the same to him.

"Then he came to me and asked: 'And how are you feeling?'"

Pain is relative—and so is how we endure it.

They say that having a kidney stone is like delivering a child.

When I say "they," I mean everyone.

I mean, I must have heard it a thousand times. It didn't make me feel any better. And I have no way of knowing that, but I do know that my stays in the hospital when my kids were born were much more pleasant than this one. For me, anyway.

Amazing things happen at the hospital. Miraculous things. Just a few months before, a congregant lay near death in one room while, just down the hall, his great-grandchild was being born.

My God! I always feel it is such a gift to be part of all that.

When I first became a rabbi, going to the hospital was hard for me. The smells, the alarms, the gyrations of hope and despair, all on the same floor, and the burden on the pastor to do something about it all, to explain the inexplicable. But I came to see these visits as gifts, as blessings.

Until that August 26.

Until I was there myself. By myself. Helpless to do anything for anyone. Helpless to take my dogs out in the storm, to bring food home, to make sure my family was safe. Helpless even to walk across the room, much less to leave that room. Unlike other times when I've been at the hospital with other family members, this time I never left the room and I kept the door closed.

So I stopped complaining. At least I tried. I left the hospital with an ample supply of pills and an appointment for lithotripsy, which shattered the stone, but the fragments did not come out. So the pain continued to govern my life in the ensuing weeks, with, given my ailment, what one might aptly call a trickle-down effect. Ethan went back to college by train because I couldn't drive him. I missed morning services for several days and a couple of shivas at night. I would take pain pills as infrequently as I could, not wanting to become too dependent on them, but I made sure to take them a couple of hours before I really needed to function. On those few occasions when I was hungry, I didn't enjoy the food because everything tasted different. I had to build up fortitude before going to the bathroom, knowing that it would involve pain.

I slept in a certain way, hoping it might reduce the pain if I woke up in the night. Every move became more calculated, each moment more mindful.

At work I was able to function as needed through some wonderful Bar and Bat Mitzvahs and a 9/11 program. Clergy tend to want illness to be a private thing. Heaven forbid, people might think we're human! But I felt it was important to be transparent about this so that inaccurate rumors wouldn't spread and also to encourage all of us never to fear openly confronting fear of illness and the reality of pain.

After all, my suffering was minuscule compared with others who have borne my title. Rabbi Nachman of Bratzlav would go to extremes to torture his body. He would fast for days on end to control hunger. Legend has it that he would roll naked in the snow to manage his physical desires (and this is without having a hot tub in the backyard). Most amazingly, he never scratched himself. Never. Anywhere.

Leviticus 16 commands us regarding Yom Kippur, "Afflict yourselves," and from the Hebrew word "afflict," we get an entire Talmudic tractate called *Ta'anit*, which describes numerous fast days prescribed by the rabbis, particularly in times of drought. The rabbis were gluttons for fast days, it seems. More pain, more gain—and more rain.

But while I talked the talk, I found it hard to walk the walk. I just couldn't go back to the hospital to visit patients. Having now been in the bed, it was hard to go back there. I had a visceral, gut response that told me to stay away. I couldn't deal with it.

It took me a couple more weeks to build up the fortitude—or, as I joked, the *stones*—to go back. When I went, it was exactly three weeks from the day I first took ill. I was just at the point where I was thinking about what steps might be required to finally pass this kidney stone. After visiting a patient, I stepped into the third-floor bathroom, summoned a pee . . . and it came out.

The stone came out in, of all places, the hospital, the very hospital where it had been first discovered.

I'm probably the only Jew on this planet who, just two weeks before Rosh Hashanah, celebrated "Pass-over."

I thought of the prayer Jews say each morning about the wondrous intricacy of the human body. I felt an immediate sense of healing and relief. And I was amazed that it almost seemed preordained that in order to get this thing behind me, I had to go back to the hospital, the place where I had felt so much pain. I had to face my demons square on. I had to overcome that revulsion and get back to the task of living, and my body responded in kind. I had to will myself to get beyond the pain.

Mensch•Mark 22

2008

NUMB AND NUMB-ER

My Task Is Not to Numb the Pain but to Highlight the Inherent Beauty of Life

I kid with dentists in my congregation that theirs is the only profession more feared than mine. And we share one other thing in common: we put people to sleep.

This past *Shavuot* (Pentecost), my congregation joined with Temple Sinai, a neighboring synagogue, for a late-night study session. When I left at the end, I was shocked to see that while we were immersed in study, a violent storm had submerged the parking lot in rippling puddles.

Here I was, at Sinai on *Shavuot*, no less, the anniversary of the giving of the Torah, and I hadn't even heard the thunder.

It's one thing to miss the Still Small Voice, the subtle miracles, but when I doze through the entire Sinaitic storm, the snapping branches and swirling leaves, I have to begin wondering whether I've been in this profession too long.

Twenty-five years ago, I stepped out into the world from Park Avenue Synagogue with the rest of my rabbinic class. From that day until this moment, I've struggled with the issue of numbness. Rabbinic lives involve a constant lurching from crisis to crisis, making it nearly impossible to hear every cry—whether human or divine—or to be completely present for any of them.

During one recent evening, I confronted the sudden deaths of a revered congregational elder and a young father in peak health. Complicating matters even more, I got the call about the young father at the precise moment when my wife and I were halfway out the door to bring our son to the same ER where he was. Thankfully, my son would be fine, but for four nightmarish hours, I shuttled from cubicle to cubicle, switching roles from rabbi to dad and back again (see Mensch•Mark 13, "Leaping with Angels"). I couldn't be there for just one. I had to be there for all. I had every excuse to ignore the congregant, who lay in a coma and whose family was in a state of utter shock. But I simply couldn't do that. Nor could I give my own child short shrift.

I had to somehow help everyone else get through while maintaining my own sanity.

Rabbis don't need pills or alcohol to become numb. Religion is the opiate of the masses, according to Marx, the great numbing agent of civilization. But Marx got it wrong. While life can be unbearable, Judaism lives in the ability of rabbis to heighten awareness, not deaden it behind comforting cure-alls, soothing stories, and pastoral balm. My role is, indeed, to be present and comfort people but not to deaden their pain.

I went to the dentist a few weeks ago for a relatively simple procedure. As soon as he entered the room, I could tell that this session would not be so routine. His troubled face startled me. I'm one of those squeamish types who see every visit to the dentist as a potential remake of *Marathon Man*.

But my teeth were not the source of his concern.

As he shot me up with Novocain, he told me about a recent trip to Lithuania and his sadness to see how the great Jewish community of Vilnius, once teeming with 105 synagogues and six daily newspapers, had in an instant been reduced to almost nothing.

What saddened him most was how non-Jews spoke with such apathy about their neighbors' fate, how they had simply taken what the Jews left behind: their silver, their homes, everything.

"Are you numb yet?" he asked me, seeking my reaction to his story.

"*Mphhh mphhh,*" I replied, which translated from numb-speak means, "Never again," or "That's why we have Israel now."

I expected him to echo those sentiments, to affirm how important it is to remain proudly Jewish in light of these tragic events, to support Israel and stand up to hatred everywhere. That's the answer I was taught in rabbinical school, the one I've been spouting for decades.

But that's not what he said.

Instead, he openly wondered why, given these seemingly inevitable results, one should remain Jewish. Why do we need to condemn ourselves to this treatment, always to be laughed at and despised? And with Israel's survival hardly a sure bet at this point, why bother? Why should he continue to subject his family to such risk when it is easy to opt out? If the Jewish presence could so easily be wiped away from the city that once was called "the Jerusalem of Lithuania," couldn't it happen here? What would the non-Jews in White Plains or Westport do if all the Jews were evicted?

Wouldn't they just take our things and move into our homes?

Why do we always have to be on the losing team?

I replied as best I could with half a mouth:

"Mphhh mphhh."

Next week, I'm taking my family to another country where Jews once flourished, another place once compared to Jerusalem from which Jews were eventually forcibly evicted: Spain. I'm sure that as I walk the labyrinthine cobblestones of Cordoba and witness the medieval grandeur of Granada, I'll lecture my kids about the miraculous, stubborn survival of the Jewish people. But will any of us truly feel the pain of those Marranos and the injustice of their loss?

I'll also think about those Jews who have given up hope, and remind myself that it is not my job to come up with glib answers to Band-Aid this wound. After twenty-five years in the rabbinate, I can't allow myself to become oblivious to either the thunder of Sinai or the still, small cry of suffering. A rabbi's job, I've learned, is not to numb the pain but to heighten awareness of life's tragic nature and the inherent beauty of survival.

"Life isn't meant to be easy; it's meant to be life," James Michener wrote at the end of *The Source*.

"But take courage," George Bernard Shaw said, describing life. "It can be delightful."

Mensch•Mark 23

GOODNESS AND MERCY

My Sudden Realization of Being "the Rabbi"

I performed my first funeral on Friday, September 17, 1982, at 2 PM, just four hours before a glorious Hudson Valley sunset would usher in my first Jewish New Year as a pulpit rabbi, though still a student. As I made my way up the Taconic from the Bronx, where I lived at the time, to my new congregation, I confronted a world of uncertainty. It was a time of great trepidation for the Jewish people: Israeli troops surrounded Beirut; synagogues throughout Europe were protected by armed guards; and here in America, demographic studies were showing an aging and shrinking Jewish population.

And now it had shrunk by one more, a woman who went by the name of Frieda Katz.

I had never met Frieda while she was alive, but I would be the rabbi to bury her. There was no one else. It had to be me. Not only that, after the burial, the synagogue president informed me that I'd need to stop at the hospital to visit another Jew, this one not a congregant, who lay near death and had requested to see a rabbi. That would be me as well.

All of this and I wasn't even a real rabbi yet.

It was my fifth and final year of rabbinical school, and students in their final year were required to do field work. Rather than doing what most of my classmates did, take cushy internships in large suburban pulpits with established rabbis, I had chosen to go it alone as a student rabbi in a small congregation in Beacon, New York, a sleepy industrial town along the Hudson, an hour and a half north of Manhattan. Fresh off my study year in Israel and newly married, I'd taken the job to support myself and my new wife, knowing that a part-time pulpit would be invaluable in honing my skills while also enabling me to decide what kind of rabbinic work I'd prefer to do after ordination. I proclaimed myself ready for prime time. So I chose Beacon, and Beacon chose me.

In Beacon, I was not only *a* rabbi, I was *their* rabbi, the latest of a string of part-time student rabbis hired to support the aging, diminishing membership of the Beacon Hebrew Alliance.

Just ninety minutes from Manhattan, the largest concentration of Jews this side of Tel Aviv, and I was the only rabbi around.

My first Shabbat there, the prior week, had been surprisingly refreshing. I'd forgotten how enjoyable it was to be out of the ivory tower of the seminary and among "real" Jews. No apologies, no discomfort, no "holier than thou" bluster coming from the group. These weren't country bumpkins, but they weren't judgmental city slickers either. They didn't expect perfection in the services I led. They weren't second-guessing my every Judaic proclamation the way my professors habitually did. I didn't need to hand in my sermons with footnotes. They were not burdened by the paralyzing fear of assimilation, for they were already totally assimilated. Their kids didn't have Hebrew names. They drove on Shabbat. They ate whatever they ate. All they wanted from me was a chance to feel Jewish again. They just wanted to connect, and I was happy to oblige. They listened to me and thought me wise. Everything seemed to be falling into place.

Until I got the call about Frieda Katz.

That had occurred the night before. I had just put the finishing touches on my first day's sermon, one with a Star Wars theme that would make me sound really cool to the twelve or so Bar Mitzvah students I would be teaching that year, except when I mistakenly said "Skyrocket" instead of "Skywalker" (the first huge embarrassment of my rabbinate; I should have framed it and hung it on my wall). The president of the congregation called to let me know about Frieda. While it was inevitable that I'd have to do a funeral sometime, I never expected it to happen this soon, and certainly not on the eve of Rosh Hashanah.

I had no chance to meet with the family until we were all at the funeral home, just minutes before the service was scheduled to begin. I knew nothing about the woman but came up with some thematic things to say, such as how Frieda, like Moses, had brought us to the brink of the Promised Land, the New Year, even though she would not be able to cross over with us. The family arrived, sobbing, and I trembled slightly as I pinned the black mourning ribbons to their clothing. We sat together and talked about Frieda so I could get to know her before I buried her. I wasn't sure what to think or feel, or whether my role was, in fact, not to feel anything but to be the balm, a source of faith and stability to stem the flow of tears.

I had spent years and years convincing myself that I would never fall so conventionally into that role, that I'd never become that caricature of a rabbi whom I had detested while growing up: the rabbi who sheds his humanness to become what others expect him to be, the rabbi who loses the ability to touch and be touched.

I felt a twang of empathy for the Katzes, and nearly cried myself, but that stemmed more from my own sense of loss and fear of failure. My father had died shockingly just a few years before—and at an already tumultuous time in my life, my first year of rabbinical school. I summoned my own grief in order to reflect back theirs. I was scared, but I couldn't show it.

But I felt nothing at all for Frieda. Frieda could just as well have been their pet dog or their hamster. She was an abstraction to me. It was such an absurd position to be the center of the entire proceeding and yet also be the only person in the room who had never met the deceased. I went through the motions, from the formulaic recitation of Psalm 23, right up to the shoveling of earth into the grave, and final prayers, just like they taught me in school.

And when it was over, when I turned to the mourners to leave, mentioning something about needing to make a quick exit to see a woman at the hospital, Frieda's husband suddenly clutched my arm and said, "You mean you're not going back to the house with us?" He had a desperate look in his eye, as if I had some strange power to heal simply by virtue of my as yet unachieved title. Or maybe it was because I seemed detached from emotion at that moment, despite my best efforts to feign pain.

I tried to rip myself away from his arm. To go. But where?

To the house? To the hospital? To the synagogue to finish my preparations for the holiest days of the year? Or back to the Bronx to curl up on my bed in a fetal position?

I looked at the husband and his damned pleading eyes. I looked at my watch. I looked at the already descending sun.

Was I ready for this?

I pulled back some more. Another question came to mind: Why was I doing this at all? What had I gotten myself into?

"Please, come back to our house," Frieda's husband implored.

They hadn't taught me about this in rabbinical school.

I resented his trying to control me. I resented his neediness. Why did it matter to him if I went back? The man didn't know me. I had barely met him. What difference could it possibly make to have me there? How could it possibly comfort him?

Then I realized. It's not "me" who mattered. He didn't want "me" to come to the house. He wanted "the rabbi." He needed "the rabbi."

I still couldn't have cared less about Frieda Katz. But Mr. Katz, whose first name I cannot recall, well, I found myself beginning to feel a pull toward him.

As I drove toward the Katz home, looking out over the lush Hudson Valley, I reflected on the valley of the shadow that I was traversing, and that twenty-third Psalm that I had just recited.

I never found "The Lord Is My Shepherd" to be a particularly comforting poem. If God is a shepherd, that makes the rest of us sheep. For Jews, especially after the Holocaust, with its pervasive imagery of the victims as sheep being led to the slaughter, we don't subscribe to the notion of being led through the valley of the shadow of death for 2,000 years simply to end up as a lamb chop on the plate of some Nazi. Jews don't make very good sheep. We tend to resent being herded and manipulated.

Plus, Psalm 23 is so well known because of its use in Christian circles, particularly Catholic. It fits in better for those whose spiritual leader, the Pope, is the embodiment of the psalmist's hero, shepherd's crook and all. Something about that psalm just didn't seem Jewish to me, even though it came right out of our Bible. But there was one aspect of the psalm that had resonated with me since early childhood.

Good Mrs. Murphy.

You know, *Good Mrs. Murphy.* She was the one who protected us from all the monsters embedded in that scary Valley of the Shadows. *That* Good Mrs. Murphy.

Surely Good Mrs. Murphy shall follow me all the days of my life.

That's the verse so many of us recited in Sunday schools of all denominations. Mrs. Murphy was as real to us as that other great school-day hero Richard Stans, to whom we would dedicate our patriotic allegiance each morning ("And to the republic, for Richard Stans . . ."). There were times when I wondered whether Mrs. Murphy would ever get married to Richard Stans, thereby creating a more perfect union of God and country. But Stans and Murphy were never destined to cross paths at my religious and public schools.

Around that time, the Jewish Publication Society (JPS) was publishing a new translation of the Bible, incorporating all the tools of modern scholarship to reconstruct in idiomatic English the original meaning of the Hebrew Bible. And they translated that pivotal verse as "only goodness and steadfast love shall pursue me all the days of my life." As for the shadow of the valley of death, it became the "valley of deepest darkness." I could live with the shadow becoming a shadow of its former self. But did they have to kill off Good Mrs. Murphy?

JPS might have, but I never did. I refused to allow Mrs. Murphy to vanish forever in the valley, and while I was at it, I resurrected the shadow. But my cup, matching the new JPS, no longer runneth over. It now overflows. When I first saw this new translation, I wondered whether the JPS team might have downed a few too many overflowing cups before daring to tinker with these immortal lines.

The psalm speaks of a maturing shepherd's yearning for the protective environment of an unrecoverable past, a past we all seek to retrieve. Good Mrs. Murphy is that past personified: that first grade teacher who wiped a runny nose or kissed a scraped knee, and the nurse or nanny who knew just when we were in the mood for a frosty glass of Nestle's Quick.

When I was a preschooler, I recall taking a nap every day from 2:20 to 4:10. How can I remember the times so exactly? Because the hands on the clock switched places, and I would be disoriented and frightened when I woke up, until I heard Good Mrs. Murphy in the other room singing a soothing Irish folk melody.

My Good Mrs. Murphys were actually named Mrs. Lanigan, my Irish babysitter from Mission Hill in Boston, Mrs. Hamburger, my kindergarten teacher, and Mrs. Hammerman, my mother. Their names weren't as important as their hands, which never let me touch a scalding stove or fall when I was trying on ice skates, and their voices, which taught me my ABCs and gently corrected me when I pinched the neighbor's cat. When deep darkness threatened, which happened every day about a half hour after sunset, Mrs. Murphy was there. I slept each night secure in the knowledge that she would follow me all the days of my life.

That's what the author of the twenty-third Psalm must have been thinking about when he wrote of his longing for God resembling the archetypal Good Mrs. Murphy, a loving, maternal deity to tuck him in.

And that's what the widower Mr. Katz needed from me.

There's nothing magical about being a rabbi. But at times of existential crises, when the valley and the darkness both appear unescapably deep, someone needs to be there to say it will be okay, even if it won't—or at least not for a long time. I understood at that moment why I needed to go back to the house and why nothing else at that moment mattered. I needed to become Good Mrs. Murphy.

I went back to the Katz house and stayed with them for as long as they needed, right up until it was time to head for services to usher in the New Year. The hospital would regrettably have to wait. Only so many people can I save in a day.

I no longer shudder when the hands of the clock switch places from 2:20 to 4:10. My clock no longer has hands. But I still search for Good Mrs. Murphy in the darkness. She no longer follows me with arms outstretched, ready to catch me if I fall. She and Richard Stans have flown away, along with my teddy bear, my blanket, and Puff the Magic Dragon.

But I know that she is out there, somewhere. And someday I'll find her again. In the meantime, thanks to her, I can bring some small amount of goodness and mercy—and steadfast love—to the lives of people who need me. If 99 percent of life is just showing up, being a rabbi has taught me that being present, even for a total stranger, can be a source of infinite grace to those in need.

I lift my overflowing cup in honor of Good Mrs. Murphy, for I discovered at my first funeral that she lives on in each of us all the days of our lives.

Mensch•Mark 24

OVER AND OUT

The Ultimate Test of Trust

Of all the funerals I've done, this was one of the most excruciating. The outing of a deceased congregant in the eulogy, at his request.

As a rabbi, I'm often called upon to do unusual things, like dressing up as a pig on Purim and as a human matzo for Passover. Destination weddings are my personal favorites. I'll go anywhere that doesn't involve skydiving or officiating close to an active wasp's nest. Very little can faze me.

But nothing prepared me for the dying congregant who asked that I out him at his funeral.

I must admit, I love doing funerals. Does that make me weird? I've done hundreds of them, for centenarians, newborns, and everyone in between. I've buried close relatives, colleagues, and friends, and I've buried people who had tried to professionally bury me. I've eulogized the famous and the destitute, with thousands present or just me and the gravedigger. I've flown to Jerusalem for a twenty-minute burial and then turned right around and flown home. I could write a Fodor's guide to every Jewish cemetery in the tristate region and every *shiva* house in Fairfield County.

It is during the confusion and craziness following a death that rituals are most needed, for they provide clarity and order. At a time when people are asking "Why?" the deft religious leader understands that they are seeking not a theology lesson but an outstretched hand and a warm embrace. The more funerals I do, the more I am able to help people through these passages. I've been there so many times that I've become a veritable GPS through the valley of the shadow of death. Without saying a word, I can assure them that it gets better. Doing so many funerals also heightens the importance of counting my days, of appreciating every moment of life. That's why even young rabbis appear to be steeped in an elder's wisdom. We experience death over and over, day after day.

With each eulogy I write, I fight the impulse to slip into clichés. I know most of the people whom I bury—one of the perks of being in one community for so long—but even when I don't know them well, I put my graduate degree in journalism to work. I sit with the family and ask probing but polite questions, and then listen closely as the key themes of the person's life emerge. Somehow the spark of divinity in each human soul must be translated into words. Somehow the narrative of that life must be imbued with transcendent meaning. It's a terrifying and awesome task, even in the most routine circumstances, not to "box in" the person in the box but instead to do justice to his or her life.

But this circumstance was hardly routine.

In late 2009, my congregant, a close friend of two decades, one who had loyally stood by my side through many of my own travails, was dying of AIDS. This discovery had forced him to disclose the truth to his inner circle but not to the world. We'll call him by his Hebrew name, Mordechai.

The Tyler Clementi suicide, precipitated by the hate-filled cyber-bullying of the Rutgers student, had a profound impact on Mordechai, leading to a series of conversations between us about how he might be able to help future Tylers face up to bullying, self-doubt, and lone-liness. He felt that if his story could save the life of just one person, something positive might come of his own suffering as well as his family's. He decided that my outing him at his funeral would be the way. But the outing had to be done carefully, not to please the gossipers with sensationalized details, but to send the right message, one that would respect his grieving family as well as his legacy.

With my encouragement, Mordechai began to write his memoirs. He didn't get too far—just seventy pages. At the funeral, I read what he wrote about his time in college:

> I was convinced that being gay would cost me my friends, my family, my ambitions. After all, who would knowingly hire a gay person? I was convinced that my parents would disown me. I was convinced that all my friends would abandon me. So with the costs so high, I did what most did: I continued to live a life in a closet of my own making and shut out my gayness until the late evening hours when I would be a gay man in search of companionship.
>
> I met so many men on those lonely evenings. And I'm con-vinced that the number of gay men living a straight life are too numerous to even speculate. I'm convinced that the number of gay people is far in excess of what the statistics say. And I'm convinced that the number of gay men who are unhappy is staggering.
>
> I couldn't give up my straight life. I hated living a double life. I knew I was gay and would have been happy to openly live a gay

life if it had been acceptable. What I wanted was to be a gay man able to live his life in a straight world but still be able and happy to be gay. I knew at that time in the 1970s that it wasn't possible. And I came to accept that my routine would just simply go on until which time I would get caught. But who would catch me? My family was a thousand miles away. So what I worried about was being a disappointment to all my friends and family should they somehow find out that I was gay. If you were gay in the 1960s and 1970s, there was a hostile society environment. So I worked really hard at my double life and told no one about my life and embarked upon living a double life in a dark and scary closet.

Mordechai lay dying just as the holiday of Purim was approaching. He was a living embodiment of the Purim story, actually. The original Mordechai and Esther also struggled with who they were and whether to reveal their true identity amid all the dangers. In the end, they did, and it saved the Jewish people. In the end, on Purim, the holiday of masks, the masks came off.

When the masks finally came off, Mordechai was not abandoned, neither by his family nor his friends. The world had changed since his youth, he discovered. It had become more accepting, despite the horrors visited on people like Tyler Clementi.

It *does* get better.

I said that at his funeral. I emphasized that while he had rolled the dice many times in his life, winning some and losing some, he did it all with courage and with love.

A few days before he died, as he could barely speak audibly while drifting in and out of consciousness, his eyes suddenly opened and he looked up at me and asked, simply, "What's it like?"

I assumed he wasn't asking what's it like to be a rabbi, for he already knew that story. He had stood with me during my most heated professional challenges. But what's it like on the other side, after death? That simple question spoke volumes about the journey Mordechai had taken. While he hadn't yet fully forgiven himself, he had begun to make his peace with God. Religion was no longer "hooey" to him, an expression he had constantly used, but something far more complicated, and his fate far more hopeful.

He then told me about an episode earlier in life when his faith was supremely challenged. When his younger daughter was an infant she became very sick and nearly died. The fact that she survived made it impossible for him to say that his life was meaningless.

I fumbled through a quasi-answer to "What's it like?" and held his hand.

"Maybe someday you'll tell *me* what it's like *there*. But I can tell you what it will be like *here*. You will be remembered with deep respect and love."

Nothing can wipe out all the pain, but by knowing that I would be telling part of his story posthumously, Mordechai found a measure of redemption.

That's what I try to do with every funeral. I resurrect dreams. Rabbi-journalist that I am, I pick up the messy manuscript of an unedited life, finish the concluding chapter, clean up the punctuation, and prepare a life story for eternal publication.

In this case, at least, as I left the cemetery, I felt that I had done justice to a noble soul—and that at last he and his family could be at peace.

Mensch•Mark 25

2013

THE VALE OF TEARS

A Condolence Call to a Place of Unspeakable Suffering

In October 2013, nearly a year after Sandy Hook, I finally made the pilgrimage to the ground zero of gun violence, a bucolic New England town just an hour's drive away from my front door. I was still grieving for my hometown of Boston, also stricken by inconceivable violence that year. On this night, the two came together, and I wondered whether there ever can be normalcy in the Vale of Tears.

Last week, I visited Newtown High School at the invitation of a congregant in her twenties who was speaking to freshmen of her struggles with alcoholism and addiction. The presentation was very moving. But here I want to share some reflections on my first visit to Newtown since the catastrophe.

Until now I had avoided going there, wishing to respect the privacy of the grieving Newtowners. But my student's invitation gave me the chance to begin to understand whether the people of Newtown, like my congregant herself, had begun to move on from their own hellish nightmare.

I took the back roads of Fairfield County, avoiding the rush hour traffic on the Merritt Parkway. With the fall foliage near peak, each twist and turn was lovelier than the last, a portrait of New England picket fence perfection. The trees were blazing in oranges and reds; the pumpkins, the Indian corn, the crispy leaves lining the driveways and surrounding mailboxes: all as deceptively peaceful as last December's snow. My GPS led me through Redding and Bethel and on to Newtown and then to the high school located in Sandy Hook.

I so wanted it all to feel normal. And I found normalcy: football games, pizza places, banners for October festivals, Halloween decorations everywhere. The high school looked like any other high school, even the enhanced security is now typical of all schools (though here I made a beeline for the security desk to let them know that this strange person with the beanie is actually the rabbi of one of the presenters).

Even this program was strangely normal. Every high school has (or should have) an evening when the police, lawyers, social workers, doctors, MADD parents, and survivors of addiction assemble before the freshman class to collectively scare the bejeebers out of them lest they ruin their lives and the lives of everyone they know. It's a rite of passage. Teen drinking is an enormous problem, don't get me wrong. But strangely, it seemed comforting to be at a program about kids and drinking, with the obligatory PowerPoint slides of crushed cars and bloody faces, with the scary statistics, with the talk about parents serving time for allowing their kids to host underage drinking parties, of date rape and endless vomiting, of teenage lives tragically cut short. All of that appeared *normal* as I sat in a room in Sandy Hook.

These kids need to be shocked into awareness, for sure. But the program is part of the expected pattern of ninth grade first semester. It comes with the acne.

And in Newtown, anything normal is by definition comforting. It reestablishes the patterns of life so life can go on. It's like gorging on platters of food during shiva or the imbibing that takes place at a wake.

So here we were, watching slides of horrific drunk driving accidents and in comparison to what they have seen with their own eyes, even these horrors seemed so prosaic, so commonplace. The banality of teen tragedy. This was a program about the needless suffering and death that *every* community suffers. Not the horrors that only one community has ever seen.

At one point, a policeman suggested that the teens should be especially careful to act responsibly "because the whole world knows where Newtown is." At first it seemed to me an unnecessary burden to place on teens striving for a return to normalcy. But it occurred to me that even the teens recognize that they will always be the subject of extra scrutiny and curiosity wherever they go. For most, I would guess, it is an emblem of pride.

I sensed a great deal of love in the room. The speakers who gave testimony, including my congregant and a young woman who had attended the high school, all received prolonged standing ovations. Many of the kids sat with parents rather than peers—no mean trick with teens—and I could only imagine the swirling emotions of parents being reminded, as if they needed a reminder, that children are vulnerable beings and that the fragility persists well beyond first grade.

This was an emotional night for me. There is so much suffering in this world, and a disproportionate amount of it has been allocated to this little corner of it. For the entire evening, I never lost awareness that I was dwelling in the valley of the shadow of death. This wasn't an ordinary high school auditorium. This is the room, after all, where the president wept. I wanted to hug everyone there but felt like an intruder, a gawker, and that my hugs would only resurrect the memories they are hoping to relegate to a lockbox in the attic.

I've been to Columbine and I've been to Wounded Knee. I've been to Boylston Street and to the Dolphinarium in Tel Aviv and Sbarro in Jerusalem. I've been to Ground Zero. I've been to Auschwitz. I've frequented many Vales of Tears. People keep living in these places. They heroically try to move on, but on some level, the tears never stop flowing. We never stop hearing the faint echoes of the victims and the *rat-a-tat-tat* or *kaboom* of the instruments of death.

And now I've been to Newtown.

I drove back home to Stamford through the misty, rainy night. I took the highway—too dark to see the foliage. No bucolic picket fences. No sparkling October sky. Just keeping my thoughts inside the car, losing myself by listening to the baseball playoffs, numbing my mind while the Red Sox comforted my grieving hometown with their pennant drive, and my wipers *swish-swished* away gallons and gallons of heaven's tears.

Mensch•Mark 26

THE TOWERS

Having the Chutzpah to Reach for the Sky

While in rabbinical school, during times when I questioned the life path I had chosen, I gained inspiration from Nikos Kazantzakis' epic memoir, Report to Greco, *and in particular this line: "God is being built. I too have applied my tiny red pebble, a drop of blood, to give Him solidity lest He perish—so that He might give me solidity lest I perish. I have done my duty."*

The idea that we are involved in the greatest construction project of all time, the building of God, suggests tremendous hubris, to be sure, but it hints at something more, capturing the spirit of chutzpah that has propelled Jewish spiritual passion into secular achievements (including 22 percent of all Nobel Prizes). The world I inhabited at my rabbinical seminary is about as far as one can get from the world of Wall Street. But a trip downtown to the sparkling new World Trade Center just after my father's death changed all that.

This essay was first written years before 2001, and then updated a few weeks after September 11, and then again in 2016.

As a child, I used to love our family trips to New York. Normally we would stay with Aunt Ruthie and Uncle Bernie in Queens. For me, New York trips meant two things: bialys and the tall buildings. I loved Aunt Ruth. She had that nasal New York accent that made me feel as if our four-hour trip had taken me to unexplored civilizations.

Ruthie always had a bag of soft, steamy bialys waiting for me when we arrived. A miracle of humankind: a bagel with half a hole. Slap on a piece of New York–style American cheese, so much sharper than the cheese up in Boston, and my mouth would water. And then there was the time she took me to the Promised Land of Manhattan. Not merely Manhattan but Macy's in Manhattan. I'll never forget that ride. I was eleven and in love with technology. The space program was big; we were just months from the moon. The Israeli Air Force had just swamped the Arabs.

And nothing glistened like New York. From the Long Island Expressway it looked like a silvery Oz edging ever closer. We sped past miles and miles of old Jewish cemeteries, the graves of my ancestors, and I hardly noticed the leaning gravestones paying homage to those taller markers in the distance. And then the store itself, each aisle fulfilling the same American dream a hundred different ways.

I came to know New York as the fulfillment of my personal American dream—a place where people from all over the world could come together, not as in a melting pot, but as coconspirators in the world's greatest Tower of Babel. Everyone striving, each on his own side of the tower, to do it bigger, better, best. It all seemed so Jewish.

In fact, the Talmudic rabbis must have had New York in mind when they looked at Genesis 11:14: "Let us build a city and a tower with its top in heaven." One midrash supposes that the builders' goal was to help hold up the firmament, evoking the image of a Jewish-style Atlas (as if God needs the help), like the one at Rockefeller Center. Another midrash claims that the Tower of Babel was an act not merely of oversized hubris but of direct military provocation against God. "'Come let us make a tower,' they say, 'and place an image on its top and a sword in its hand; and it will seem that it is waging war against God.'" In the sages' eyes, this tower's tip must have appeared like the phallic extremity of the Empire State Building.

In New York, even the non-Jews act like Jews. To me that was amazing, coming from Boston, where most of the Jews try to act like Brahmins and eat their golf ball–sized bagels with pinkies held high. Bagels don't go well with tea and scones.

Here, even the aristocracy is Jewish, or at least acts it. All the original languages and native dress are still there, but as soon as foreigners learn the native ways, they all begin to talk like Aunt Ruthie, ruminate like Woody Allen, and push even harder to reach God. New York is messianism's primary port of call.

New Yorkers meet on the public square of Jewish perfectionism, whether it be on the stages of Broadway and Lincoln Square or the court of Madison Square, in the classroom laboratories of City College or Columbia, at East Side museums and downtown Bohemian cafes. Everyone is a Prometheus with guilt, schlepping that rock up the side of the Empire State because Mom would have wanted us to because Grandma made her do it. No matter the language, even the Syrian, Korean, and Albanian find their common space on the periphery of that great bagel hole on the Hudson. And they meet over bagels while discussing how to make taller buildings, buy luckier lottery tickets, find cheaper bargains, and wear snazzier clothes. Always bigger, better, best.

If we can beat God here, we can beat God anywhere.

Beat God . . . or build God.

One winter's day while I was attending rabbinical school in the early '80s, I decided to make a pilgrimage to the World Trade Center. I was mourning my father at the time and fulfilling one of his final requests: that I purchase my own set of the Talmud. My aunts and uncles, including Aunt Ruthie, had pooled together a few hundred dollars to make possible that acquisition of twenty huge volumes of transcribed academy discussions that took place in Babylonia almost twenty centuries ago. Babylonia "and," actually: Babylonia and Israel; Babylonia and Spain; Babylonia and the Rhine Valley; Babylonia and Vilna; Babylonia and Joe's *Cooffee* Shop on 57th and *Toid*. The Talmud is the collection of the Jewish people's red pebbles, sorted and accumulated like stacks of old baseball cards in the basement, torn and reshuffled, gaining value as the teams relocate, as each generation of players dies and is enshrined in the Hall of Fame.

The Talmud by way of the Twin Towers seemed the right way to go. From the financial district, it was walking distance to the Lower East Side by way of Chinatown. The entire world and centuries of striving could be navigated within a few city blocks, or a few aisles at Macy's. Accumulated dreams. That's what I've always loved about New York.

If New York is to traditional culture a grand Temple of Audacity, the World Trade Center was its Holy of Holies. For the immigrants it was the Statue of Liberty that inspired blasphemy, she of the immodest bodily exposure, the chutzpah to study books, and the unnaturally sculpted nose. Jews liked that, and they also liked the fact that they could shed their beards here, lest they be pulled, discard their Yiddish and their Sabbath, but keep their bagel and their sense of irony as they pushed their way up the ladder. For my generation, the Twin Towers picked up where Lady Liberty left off.

I rode to the top and was entranced by the view. Looking out, psalms appeared in my mind. The rivers were frozen gray meandering ribbons, the Palisades looked like children's slides. The Catskills lay as panting dogs below me in the distance. There the jagged Chrysler, here the sharp-stepped Empire, and beyond, the mighty UN, a massive bookend holding the East River in its place. The rivers may have been clogged arteries, but the bridges glistened from the same snow as trucks edged along them delivering life to the periphery. Directly ahead, the traffic copters skipped like rams from cloud to cloud.

The exhibit at the top was, appropriately, on the history and future of world trade. It boldly predicted a time not far off, around the year 2000, when nations would effectively give way to a new multinational order, where almighty capitalism would unite us all in the pursuit of happiness. It predicted major technological advancements in almost every realm. Communications would be instant and global. Leisure time would be increased exponentially. Disease would be defeated; cloning would be commonplace. In less than two centuries, a cure for death itself would be found. Immortality, at last, would be ours. God would be out of business.

In Genesis 11:6, God frets over the Tower of Babel, saying, "Here, one people with one language for them all, and this is merely the first of their doings—now there will be no barrier for them in all that they scheme to do."

Like God in Genesis, I was shaken by these predictions. If God were out of business, I feared, I was in the wrong profession myself. I decided to leave the Wall Street region quickly and bought a bagel on the ground floor to energize myself for the cold crosstown trek to the bookstore on Essex Street. First the faces changed, from the coiffed and choreographed, moussed, nose-hair tweaked, and white-shirted Wall Streeters, through the many shapes and smells of Chinatown, to the craggy, ancient, dusty black frock of the *s'forim* (holy book) salesman at H and M Skullcap. He, too, had to climb a tower, well, a ladder, to a warehouse loft where the Vilna editions of the Talmud were kept.

He showed me several varieties. I chose one with a yellow cover and on it the design of, incredibly, a tower. It looked like an ancient Roman ruin of some sort, with two roaring lions at the front. Well, not exactly roaring. These looked like Jewish lions, sort of like my grandfather Shloime, in fact, and they were more *kvetching* than roaring.

But it was a tower nonetheless. And I began to understand that, despite the yawning gap of time and milieu, a culture shock you get in New York every three blocks, things were not that different after all. What was the Talmud but another Babylonian tower, another edifice intended not to usurp God but to engage in an innocent and noble stretching of limits? A classic Talmudic tale is of a rabbi who over-rules the voice of God in making a key legal decision. The other rabbis are compelled to agree, and God is heard to say, up in the heavens, most likely with great pride, "My children have defeated me! My children have defeated me!" This was hardly a hostile takeover. Hubris is tragic only when translated into Greek. Jews call it "chutzpah," and God seems to love it.

Twenty years after this visit, I came to realize that the World Trade exhibit didn't have it all wrong: cloning was a reality, communications had become instantaneous, the Soviet Union was gone, and national realignments were being based primarily on economic considerations. Yet the role of religious tradition was also strengthening.

No need to be threatened by the strivings of technology, I figured. Let them strive to defeat death in their way and me in mine, them with their edifice of exploration and me with my tower of tradition. All the towers can coexist in New York only a few blocks apart.

I left the bookstore and crossed Essex Street for a fresh bialy at Kossars. At that point, standing amid the babble of what seemed like a dozen immigrant cultures crammed into this one creaky corner of the Manhattan melting pot, I realized that no matter where I went, even up to the top of the world, the whole city smelled like bagels.

Now in my post–September 11 grief, I've come to realize that in fact the Towers of the West Side were the bookends that kept my Lower East Side *s'forim* safely on the shelf. And I wonder, with great sadness, will we ever strive to climb that high again?

Addendum

In the summer of 2016, I made a pilgrimage to the 9/11 Memorial Museum, my first such visit since it was completed. Part of the museum is dedicated to tracing the roots of the hatred that would drive normal human beings to such rabid insanity as to murder thousands of innocents in cold blood. To stand at that subterranean spot, deep within the footprint of the Towers, inhaling the sacred dust bearing the pulverized bones of 2,753 victims, is a shattering experience. But it is only the beginning of the journey.

After visiting the memorial, I ascended to the top of the Freedom Tower, and there took in a view that I hadn't seen since a year before 9/11, when I performed a wedding at Windows on the World, the swanky restaurant that stood atop the North Tower. There was no view like it back then, and now we've reclaimed our corner of the sky.

As I looked out from my Freedom Tower perch in mid-August, it occurred to me that the heavens were as deep blue as on that fateful September day fifteen years before. Or at least as I recall it. An entire wall of the 9/11 Memorial Museum is filled with ceramic tiles in various shades of blue, the color of that sky as conjured through the dusty memory of those who saw it. No one can recall the exact shade, and the shade itself shifted, but it is simply remembered as the bluest blue people had ever seen; a blue that was soon eclipsed by billows of black smoke and ash funneling through the human canyons.

The Midrashic collection Sifrei Numbers, in describing the elusive blue fringe designed to help Jews remember the commandments, explains the symbolism of that color: "A thread of blue: blue like the sky, blue like the sea, blue like the divine throne."

Centuries ago, Jews stopped trying to recall that exact shade and abandoned the blue thread altogether—though now some have revived the custom—but for 9/11 survivors, which to a degree all of us are, that deep blue sky remains an important touchstone, something to help us raise our eyes heavenward again to hope, to climb, and to envision the kind of harmony that only God can imagine, something to remind us of the peacefulness and order that existed at the dawn of that day.

As I looked out a hundred floors above the pulverized dust of memory, death, and reconstruction, it occurred to me that the blue has returned.

The city lay before me, a unified patchwork of neighborhoods and jagged skyscrapers, nurtured by bridges and waterways, this enormous living organism, guarded by a lady with a lamp. It took my breath away. The city as one, organic, unified whole, greater than the sum of its extraordinary and unique parts.

In his novel *Winter's Tale*, which describes similar vistas as viewed from the back of a magical flying horse, Mark Helprin writes, "In the eyes of God, all things are interlinked." This view from the Freedom Tower, as the one from the departed Twin Towers, is truly a God's eye view. While we see the same view all the time on TV, courtesy of helicopters and blimps and planes descending to JFK and La Guardia, it's been fifteen years since I had been able to stand on elevated terra firma and with my own eyes look out from the tallest building in a city of towers, standing in the spot where the city began and where it nearly ended, from where you can look north and take in the entirety of this enchanted island.

A decade and a half later, we've dared to climb again. And we've reclaimed our corner of the sky.

THE QUESTION OF RELIGION
An Interpretation of Psalm 97

"Those who love Adonai shun evil,
so that the One who guards the spirit of kindness
will save them from bad influences."

The question of religion today
Is not how those who love God shun evil
But how those who perpetrate unlimited evil
Can do it so freely in the name of God.

We affirm, like the psalmist,
That to love God
Is to embrace kindness.

To be religious
Is to see godliness, not only in God
But in all of God's creatures

Including the other,
Including the enemy,
The one who perverts God's name in God's name.

To love God is to shun hatred
And to love all God's creatures;
But not at all costs.

To love God
Is to protect innocence
At all costs.

—*Rabbi Joshua Hammerman*

PART FIVE

Belonging and Becoming

*. . . In which we explore the many
dimensions of connection, including
nontraditional ones, the ever-shifting
boundaries of identity and observance,
and the crying need to cultivate
inclusiveness. Rabbi Donniel Hartman
writes that what makes a Jew a Jew is
the synthesis of belonging and becoming, an
amalgamation of peoplehood and principle. But in
all cases, ultimately the goal is to connect. And the
human rabbi does just that, echoing E. M. Forster's
famous cry: "Only connect!"*

"He drew a circle that shut me out—
Heretic, rebel, a thing to flout.
But love and I had the wit to win:
We drew a circle and took him In!"

—Edwin Markham

Piglet sidled up to Pooh from behind.
"Pooh?" he whispered.
"Yes, Piglet?"
"Nothing," said Piglet, taking Pooh's hand.
"I just wanted to be sure of you."

—A. A. Milne, Winnie-the-Pooh

Mensch•Mark 27

THE YARMULKE BIN

An Unassuming Beanie Became a Souvenir from Sinai

The yarmulke is not found in the Bible, and Jewish law does not require wearing one. So what can that ubiquitous beanie teach us about identity?

It is time to reflect on our most underrated and ubiquitous ritual item: the *yarmulke*.

On the surface, it seems to pale when compared with other objects. Unlike the *tallit*, it has no foundation in the Torah and law; unlike the *siddur*, it can be tossed into the garbage. It has long been the butt of jokes, partly because it sounds more like a Japanese motorcycle than a ritual garment, but mostly because our ambivalence regarding the yarmulke mirrors our ambivalence about Judaism itself.

A Jew is instantly identified when wearing one, exposed not only as a Jew but as a pious one. Some say the name stems from the Aramaic expression *Yiray Malka*, "fear of the king," based on a Talmudic anecdote that Rav Huna never walked four cubits with his head uncovered because "the Divine Presence is always over my head."

But it's more about identity than humility. Years ago, *kippah* choices were limited to the tightly stitched head huggers of traditional Zionists, the black velvet of the fervently Orthodox, and the cheap satin blends found in the typical synagogue bin. But now, as with the rest of contemporary Judaism, one size no longer fits all, and there's been an explosion of variety. You've got the colorful fez-like Bukharian and brightly colored Ethiopian models, pastel and lace feminine styles featuring embroidered gold wire and beads, the camouflaged olive suede of the IDF, the thick-knitted ski caps favored by Breslovers and other mystics, handsome silk and leather folk art options, and an infinite variety of woven styles.

There is a *yarmulke* for every taste, every ideology, and every hairline. Yeshiva students tend to like it to flop on the side, while many middle-aged men put it directly over the bald spot, like a knitted toupee. Some choose clips or Velcro to hold it in place, while others, like me, go for the subtler bobby pin.

Although they are often mass produced, each *yarmulke* tells a unique story. What other ritual item can be found in the glove compartment of nearly every Jewish-owned car? Whenever I visit a mourner's home, a basketful of *yarmulkes*, collected from every cranny of the house, invariably greets me by the door. So while we are saying *Kaddish* for Grandpa Joe, we're wearing the *kippah* (Hebrew for *yarmulke*) from Joe's wedding or from granddaughter Lucy's Bat Mitzvah or baby Evan's bris. A family's heritage literally unfolds before us as we stretch these crumpled cloths over our scalps. A *yarmulke* museum could easily be constructed within nearly every Jewish home.

My personal history can be traced in my own overflowing *yarmulke* drawer. Several of my favorites feature my Hebrew name; some were made by girlfriends. I still have *kippot* (plural of *kippah*) purchased in Jerusalem on a summer teen tour, at a time when my Jewish juices gushed so powerfully that I seriously considered wearing one all the time. I did it for a short while when I got back home, but before long, facing overwhelming pressure to conform in my public high school, I shifted back to bareheadedness. Still, I kept a *kippah* in my pocket at all times, which, I suppose, prepared me for a career in the rabbinate.

Now the crown rests more easily on my head than it did at the beginning of my career, although I still don't wear it every waking moment. I recognize it for the powerful statement that it is—and for the superficial bumper sticker it can easily become. As proud as I am to display my loyalties, I strongly resist all labels. Still, I feel much more comfortable wearing a *kippah* on a New York subway than, say, my Red Sox cap.

My kids, of course, have an ample supply of Red Sox *kippot*, plus Pokémon, Superman, Harry Potter, Big Bird, and Barney the dinosaur. Ironically, the attire designed to promote Jewish distinctiveness now enables our kids better to blend with the trendy. But that blending also enables them to become more comfortable in their Jewish skin. The *kippah*, no longer an embarrassment, now signifies "Jewish cool."

Every *kippah* tells a story.

Once when visiting with sixth graders, I grabbed the *yarmulke* storage bin from the closet and randomly picked out three to hand to some bareheaded students. Each *kippah* told a story of a Jewish journey. One was from the 1979 Bar Mitzvah of a student whose child is now in the school. A second was from a Bat Mitzvah in 1999, but it took place in New City, about an hour away. I wondered just how many heads that *kippah* had covered during its eight-year sojourn from Rockland County.

I reached for the third *kippah*. What exotic tales would it tell? Perhaps it was a mint-condition beanie from Steven Spielberg's

Bar Mitzvah, now undoubtedly worth millions on eBay! Or maybe a lipstick-stained souvenir from Arthur Miller's wedding to Marilyn Monroe. Or even the one whipped out by Menachem Begin on the White House lawn with Carter and Sadat.

I slowly unfolded *kippah* number three. Turned out it was from my own son's Bar Mitzvah. Not worth much on eBay, perhaps. But priceless to me.

The *yarmulke* bin is a time capsule documenting our intertwined destinies and most personal life choices, a portal to Jewish Narnia, a mysterious hamper filled with our most sacred laundry, overflowing with fantasy, history, and imagination.

The *kippah* is a touchstone to our holiest moments, reminding us perpetually: "Under me lived a Jew."

In the glove compartment of every Jewish car sits a souvenir from Sinai.

Mensch•Mark 28

BAR MITZVAH NATION

"They Like Us! They Really Like Us."

The current trend among thought leaders is to laugh at the foibles of the American Bar Mitzvah and call for its demise. But, as usual, the elites aren't hearing the rest of us, and Bar Mitzvah is as strong as ever. I am continually amazed at the enduring power of this rite of passage as a key indicator of how successfully Judaism can compete in the marketplace of religions.

When we look back years from now, historians might decide that Sunday, April 25, 2004, was the proverbial tipping point when all of America became Jewish.

On that evening, as Americans sat down to their nightly TV ritual, Krusty became Bar Mitzvah. For those who aren't among the nearly ten million who watch *The Simpsons*, Krusty, the rabbi's kid-turned-clown, metaphorically represents the tragi-comic Jewish condition. In this episode, Krusty, estranged from his traditionalist father (voiced by Jackie Mason), finally understands that one cannot be a Jew in name only. Seeking to earn his place among such Jewish luminaries as Sandy Koufax, Woody Allen, and Lamb Chop, Krusty decides to take a hiatus from his show to do some serious grappling with traditional texts.

My jaw dropped when I saw this. I'm more than a casual watcher of *The Simpsons* (principally because just about every Bar Mitzvah student is able to quote it chapter and verse), so when I tuned in, I was expecting the same old shtick for Krusty's Bar Mitzvah, an updated version of the excesses of *Goodbye, Columbus*. It started out that way, but ended up with Krusty headed on a serious Jewish journey.

The entire country seems to be on a Jewish journey these days.

If you got tired of Krusty on that Sunday evening in late April, you could have clicked onto *Comedy Central's Bar Mitzvah Bash*. And several weeks ago, the *Wall Street Journal* ran an article entitled "You Don't Have to Be Jewish to Want a Bar Mitzvah," detailing the growing trend of non-Jewish children begging their parents for big Bar/Bat Mitzvah bashes of their own. When non-Jews can so casually assimilate what has long been the decisive generator of Jewish identity, it makes us wonder what sort of monster we've created.

A successful monster, that's what.

Think about it. Mainstream America is now so completely comfortable with Judaism that it can dabble in overtly Jewish symbols without denying their Jewishness. These kids aren't clamoring for mere parties but for Bar Mitzvahs. Without batting an eye, they are choosing to live within the framework of Jewish idiom. All we have to do is add content and stir. Certain Jewish values are already built into even the most secularized and over-the-top Bar Mitzvah: the love of family, for instance. But the hard work has already been done. From a marketing perspective, Bar Mitzvah is becoming the Coca-Cola of

American adolescent initiation rites. "Want to celebrate your coming of age? Have a Bar Mitzvah and a smile—it's *real.*"

The most amazing thing is happening: non-Jews are teaching Jews how to be Jewish.

It used to be that Hollywood was filled with Jews pretending to be non-Jews, lining up to change their names from Goldfish to Goldwyn and from Birnbaum to Burns. Now the entire non-Jewish branch of the entertainment industry is going gaga over Kabbalah, which *W* magazine recently called "Hollywood's trendiest spiritual movement since A.A." I remain wary of the kind of hucksterism that threatens to sever Kabbalah from its authentic Judaic roots (the Kabbalah Center purportedly sells those red-yarn bracelets for $26, a rip-off, even if Britney Spears did wear one on the cover of *Entertainment*). But there is nothing inherently evil about being trendy.

When Madonna proclaims, as she recently did, that she will no longer do concerts on Shabbat, something profound is happening here. The singer announced through her publicist that she would instead be attending services on Friday evenings. The Jewish establishment scoffs at these statements when we should be embracing them. I doubt we would take Madonna seriously even were she to shorten her name to "Maidl," but we who have been preaching the merits of Shabbat all these years to those few who will listen between the yawns have quite a bit of chutzpah (a word you can now look up in your *American Heritage Dictionary,* where it has been accepted into English) to pooh-pooh the cultural earthquake that is going on around us.

Hello, my name is Josh, and I am a recovering pooh-pooher.

I needed to make that confession because for years I've come down hard on the superficiality of American Judaism. It was the *Titanic*-themed Bat Mitzvah party in Pittsburgh with the iceberg centerpiece that threw me overboard. So it was natural for me to perceive the shallowness of those who pose with red thread. But I've grown more tolerant since then. Two months ago, my eldest child, Ethan, made his Sinaitic climb to the bima, and as I watched his Jewish destiny begin to unfold, I experienced for the first time as an adult the full power of the Bar Mitzvah rite. Even in America. *Especially* in America.

I know how powerful Judaism can be, which is why I take Madonna seriously. She may not be Jewish—yet—but she is living, increasingly, a Jewish life. She's even doing a concert tour of Israel this fall, and the morale boost Israelis will feel will be as real as the mitzvah she is performing. Madonna has a long way to go, but at least she is headed in the right direction: East. I guess you don't have to be Jewish to be a good Jew. Demi Moore, of all people, put it best: "I didn't grow up Jewish, but I would say that I've been more exposed to the deeper meanings of particular rituals than any of my friends that did."

As we celebrate 350 years of Jewish presence on these shores, some strange things are happening. While Jews have been focusing all our attention on Mel Gibson's controversial film *The Passion*, some of our neighbors have become mighty passionate about Judaism. New forms of Jewish expression are attracting Americans in droves. As they say in Hollywood, "They like us! They really like us!" Maybe Krusty's Bar Mitzvah can mark a turning point for us, too.

Mensch•Mark 29

2 0 1 0

MY FATHER'S HUPPAH

A Catholic Tevye and the Brave New World of Assimilation

Fiddler on the Roof has officially gone the way of the bagel and the word chutzpah. It belongs to everyone now. But has its message been unalterably changed? And if so, is that change for the better?

The questioner was an African American high school student, not Jewish, playing the role of Tevye's daughter Chava in an astonishingly multicultural production of *Fiddler on the Roof*, one that brought together more than one hundred students of all ages from twenty-four private and public schools in my modern Anatevka. Thanks to my son Dan, cast as Nachum the Beggar, I was asked to be the show's rabbinic adviser.

"Rabbi, why does Tevye act like his daughter is dead when she marries someone who isn't Jewish? Is that what Jews do?"

I had just watched them rehearse the wedding scene and couldn't help but be struck by the irony of a Catholic Tevye and a Catholic Golda serenading their African American and Asian daughters with "Sunrise, Sunset," while a Hispanic rabbi, a recent immigrant from Colombia, performed the ceremony; and lurking in the background, a Jewish Cossack waited for his cue to wreak havoc on this bucolic scene.

At the center of the stage was the very symbol of Jewish continuity, the wedding canopy. And not just any canopy but my father's small faded linen huppah, off-white with gold tassels, embroidered gold flowers on the sides, and a simple Jewish star on top. The four stubby wooden poles covered with peeling gold cloth give it a kitschy look, like something rescued from a Catskills catering hall, last seen in faded photos alongside the chopped liver and gefilte fish. My father had used this huppah when performing small private weddings before stashing it in the attic sometime before his sudden death thirty years prior. There it remained in a crumpled pile until my mother and I rediscovered it when we were packing up the house. I had it cleaned and pressed, and since then my father's huppah has graced a number of weddings I've performed.

But up until that moment when I sat there watching this *Fiddler* rehearsal, only Jews had stood underneath it.

A Catholic Tevye? Sounds crazy, no?

Imagine a production of *1776* performed by Iranian mullahs, *Hair* by octogenarians, or *Rent* by Republicans. But somehow, this all-school *Fiddler* worked. This dizzying production challenged some of my deepest held convictions, forcing me to play a Tevye-like role in a twenty-first-century sequel, prodding me to calibrate what God might expect of us in an age of radical global shrinkage and swiftly dissolving boundaries.

Tevye, the Shalom Aleichem character, would never have allowed this Tevye, the Trinity Catholic student, to marry his fictional daughters. And the majority of the actors playing the daughters would themselves have been banned from standing under the huppahs of the real-life *shtetls* where those fiddlers fiddled. But there they were, at center stage, standing under mine.

The cast members peppered me with detailed questions about lighting candles, kissing mezuzahs, and spitting to ward off the evil eye. I sensed from this very diverse group of students a desire to wrap their arms around their characters and make them their own. They wondered why it was seen as so radical for girls to dance with boys and whether Yenta still exists ("JDate," I replied). Somehow this production of *Fiddler* made perfect sense to them, and because of that, it began to make sense to me as well, as it likely would have to Shalom Aleichem himself, a man who embraced life's absurdities, saying, "No matter how bad things get, you got to go on living, even if it kills you."

The wedding canopy has long been a great symbol of both exclusivity and inclusivity. It represents the home—the Jewish home—the couple will build together. In the Bible, the term connotes the private chamber where the marriage was consummated; today it still marks that sacred space reserved for bride and groom alone.

But it's also said to be modeled after Abraham's tent, which had open walls and welcomed all comers, dissolving boundaries between private and public, promoting an inclusiveness that is both intimate and ultimate.

Back in the '60s, the closest my father came to officiating at an intermarriage was something involving fans of the Red Sox and Yankees. As a justice of the peace, he often performed small weddings in my home, both for Jewish and non-Jewish couples. I was too young at the time to care which of these weddings were of the shotgun variety; my curiosity was limited by the bifurcated universe I inhabited, preoccupied with one question only: Jewish or "goyish?" If the guy wore a yarmulke, bingo! A Jewish wedding! Chalk up another one for our team!

But the huppah was always the most definitive clue. When my dad took it out of the closet, I knew it would be a Jewish ceremony. When he did not, it was not. Life was very simple back then.

But not anymore.

"Do Jews still mourn with sackcloth and ashes when their kids intermarry?"

No, I told Chava. No one does that anymore. Even Tevye wouldn't if he were alive today. I explained, as sensitively as possible, how Jews have always seen immortality less in terms of their own souls' ascent to heaven as in their children and grandchildren carrying on the faith. But Jews also want to be welcoming, like Abraham was.

Would I sit shiva for my child if he married out? Would I officiate at his wedding?

No and no.

But would I celebrate?

In the words of the immortal dairyman: I'll tell you . . . I don't know.

But I know that, like Abraham, I will love anyone who comes into my home with an unconditional, unbounded love. I'll do it because it is precisely that kind of love that will bring renewed vitality to the Jewish people and eternal relevance to the Jewish message.

And I'll do it because, as I'm sure Tevye would agree, loving our neighbor is a tradition, for it reminds us who we are and what God expects us to do.

Mensch•Mark 30

2011

JEWS OF THE JUNGLE

Lessons from the Cruel and Supremely Tranquil Savannah

Experiencing an African safari as a grand garden of Eden, though violent and cruel, left me with a deep sense of tranquility.

Last summer, I journeyed far from the daily craziness of rabbinic life to the wilds of Africa, and it was out there that I rediscovered why I do what I do back here.

Job states, "God teaches us from the animals of the land," and on safari I found myself immersed in a vast, orderly ecosystem where, Anatevka-like, all creatures know who they are and what God expects them to do. It took my breath away.

In our world, the only sure things are death and taxes. But there, the only sure thing is death. Because death is ever-present, it is strangely beautiful. Every moment is sharpened. The sunset's reds are redder, the lion's roar is louder, and the stars are unbelievably bright. Life develops its own intensified rhythm.

The animals I saw were free and content (except for those unfortunate moments when they were being eaten). They became my new congregation, often resembling the folks back home in unexpected ways.

Take the lion, for instance.

Karen Blixen wrote, "You know you are truly alive when you're living among lions." There is such pathos to their story. No wonder lions have become a prime symbol of the Jewish people and Jerusalem. So powerful, yet so fragile. Adult males wander vast distances and often appear forlorn and threatened, sharing with the Jew both nobility and mobility.

In Jewish art, lions are always guarding something; they are the epitome of earthly courage. Leon Uris chose the name Ari—lion—for his quintessential Israeli hero in *Exodus*, and Israel often uses lion synonyms in naming jet fighters.

With lions, as with Jews, the problem of continuity is particularly acute. Three out of four cubs do not make it to adulthood, and the population has become dangerously small. It was shocking to learn that lion males destroy the cubs of other sires in order to give their own kids a competitive advantage.

Back home we call that the college admissions process.

One morning we came upon two panting lions devouring a giraffe. Even this longtime vegetarian was transfixed at this most carnivorous sight, one that somehow reaffirmed my faith in the order of things. This was a meaningful death, meant to perpetuate the grand plan. That giraffe had been born, in part, for the purpose of being eaten by that lion, and on some level the giraffe knew it.

That evening, I heard the news about the mass murder that took place at a summer camp in Norway, a senseless killing in a world gone mad. In contrast, the carnage I saw on the savannah reaffirmed a grander plan and sustained nature's precious balance. I wished I didn't have to go back to "civilization."

Incidentally, did you know that giraffes are kosher? But you won't find much giraffe meat at Fairway. There are, shall we say, logistical problems. Imagine this elderly rabbi with a knife walking up to a giraffe with a stepladder and trying to find the right spot to kill it painlessly.

I fell in love with giraffes, clearly the most Jewish animal in the bush. They're basically pacifist, but they have a good swift kick to fend off predators. Like Jews, they hang out in family groups and protect one another; they are a little goofy and try to keep out of everyone else's way. And they are ruminants. That, along with the split hoof, is what makes them kosher.

It's great to be a ruminant. Giraffes get to enjoy life. They nosh a little, and then they just hang while they regurgitate their food and eat it again with their second stomach. Elephants, in contrast, have only one stomach, so they have to keep eating nonstop, daily consuming leaves and branches the weight equivalent of three people. An elephant may never forget, but memory alone is not enough. Ruminants get to, well, ruminate. Like Jews. You are what you eat, and Jews eat animals that are peace-loving ruminators.

At one point our guide alerted us to a pair of giraffes that looked like they were about to mate. We watched for several minutes. The male kept on chewing. Ruminating. Finally the female walked away. The moment was missed. God knows what this male was thinking. If giraffes are the most Jewish of animals, we had just met the Woody Allen of giraffes.

Rhinos are fascinating. Whenever I saw one I felt like we were in Jurassic Park. I asked our guide, "Who is the rhino's most feared predator?"

"You," he said.

Sure enough, rhino poaching has reached epidemic proportions in Africa. I also learned that rhino males pile their dung in huge heaps to leave a sort of calling card on their territory so their families can find them. Our guide compared the practice with posting on someone's Facebook wall. I reflected on all the dung that flies in the turf wars that so often rip apart Jewish communities. At least the rhinos pile theirs neatly.

Despite spasms of violence, most of what we saw was like a grand garden of Eden. Lots of moms and babies cuddling. Lots of eating, drinking, sleeping, and reproducing. The miracle of the ordinary. On Shabbat afternoon, I gazed down at the water hole beneath my porch and saw a small antelope gently picking at branches and drinking. I thought of Psalm 42: "As a deer thirsts for water, so, O Lord, do I thirst for You." The world around me seemed so at peace and complete. I had tapped into the great Source of all connection and Oneness. It was much bigger than me. But in part because of that, it was of great comfort. Long after I am gone, I thought, this will still be here, and to the degree that I am one with it, so will I.

It was hard to leave this blissful place. As our Jeep drove out, heading on the bumpy road toward the airport, a rhino stood by the road staring at us as if saluting us and saying good-bye. They had invited us into their world and we became a part of it. I had become the accidental non-tourist. I had tapped into the We of Me.

I thought of what Karen Blixen wrote in *Out of Africa*:

> If I know a song of Africa, of the giraffe and the African new moon lying on her back, of the plows in the fields and the sweaty faces of the coffee pickers, does Africa know a song of me? Will the air over the plain quiver with a color that I have had on, or the children invent a game in which my name is, or the full moon throw a shadow over the gravel of the drive that was like me, or will the eagles of the Ngong Hills look out for me?

My week on the savannah reminded me that I have a role to play, that I'm a small piece in a very large puzzle, that I fit in, right next to the lion and the giraffe, the Bar Mitzvah student and the grieving widow. We all have our sacred task in this eternal game.

We all know a song of Africa.

Mensch•Mark 31

1997

THE WALL AND
THE MALL

Where Is God Truly Found?
What Makes a Place "Holy"?

In all my years as a rabbi, there's only one place where Jews would not let me lead my group in prayer: at the Western Wall. Two decades later, this sacred place, which should bring Jews of differing backgrounds together, instead continues to drive them apart, now more than before. But Jews have found other venues where unity can be forged.

As an American patriot, I take immense pride in how my behemoth nation has colonized the universe with its cultural assets. Pax Americana has now even reached Mars, having long since overrun earthly Jerusalem. But as I set out on a recent visit to Israel, mindful of growing complaints of "Americanization" by my Israeli friends, I was anxious to find new evidence of the Great Satan's work. And indeed,

I didn't have to look far to find the ugliest aspects of my complicated country: the Western Wall.

The Kotel I encountered last month was as stratified as a Greenwich country club. This was not the Kotel I had first encountered as a teen twenty-four years prior on Tisha B'Av, when I was one weeper among the multitudes. The chanting of Lamentations that summer evening, the drone of a single coalescing murmur of anguished trope in and above the plaza, made for a communion of tear-swept flesh and stone. Beyond that, what struck me was the curious asymmetry of the place: sprawling stones reaching both down and upward, touched by unkempt clumps of moss, topped by smaller bricks carved by dreams of another era, topped by, of all things, a field of TV antennae. Though mundane in normal use, these masses of wire seemed apt here, a reminder that the Kotel—and God—exist on the plane of normal human experience.

In ancient times, the Kotel was the Temple's outer retaining wall, the place where all the people could gather, from the largest to the smallest, sheep and pigeons in hand, before arriving at the inner courtyards, where degrees of separation set in. The Kotel has always been a festival of earthy democracy for the plain folk: the sweaty Herodian-era laborers who moved enormous slabs of rock, the late-Roman period artisan who scribbled joyous graffiti from Isaiah, the dying whispers of medieval pilgrims having reached their long-sought final destination, the teary paratroopers in '67, the final breath of my grandmother who never got there.

When I first came to Kotel that Tisha B'Av, the fast day memorializing the destruction of the temple, I saw a white dove about halfway up, glowing in the light and perched on a nest of moss. I quivered with recognition of the *Shechina*, God's most manifest and loving presence, sent to that very spot to weep with her people among the ruins. For centuries that legend and that weeping bound motionless stones to a yearning nation.

Enter the Great Satan. Now the TV antennae are gone and the plaza is as clean and symmetrical as ever. Its aesthetic beauty is unquestioned, like the eighteenth hole at Augusta, but the sanitized Wall has lost its wail, like a Disneyfied Times Square. The plaza has also lost its democratic ardor, having become as foreigner-friendly as Syria. A decade ago, I had no problem bringing groups of congregants to the middle of the plaza, men and women together, for Friday evening services, after which we would approach the Wall as individuals to share in the euphoric cacophony of singing Yeshiva students, tourists, new immigrants, worn pilgrims, curious seekers, and long-lost friends from the States. At the Wall, the Jewish body beat with one heart.

Now the stones have lost their heart and strangers beware. On Friday night, the hugs and singing have been replaced by a stony silence and a level of suspicion worthy of a Manhattan subway. My group could not pray together, else we risk a garbage pelting. So we prayed on the newly excavated steps facing the Southern Wall. When we reached the Kotel afterward, no one embraced us. No one asked if we needed a place for Shabbat, as so many had years ago. Small cantons of ultra-Orthodox Jews prayed in pantomime; we kept our distance, hoping for a spiritual trickle-down effect.

About twenty feet from the Wall, an updated version of *West Side Story* was being played out. A dozen Reform Jews from Miami, all men, defiantly sang "*Lecha Dodi*" in a circle while ultra-Orthodox Jews stared and caucused, figuring out what to do with them. One slipped dangerously close to the group, bending over to investigate the photocopied prayer booklet, as if examining a lettuce for bugs. The Reform service concluded. Triumphantly, they had reclaimed their piece of the rock.

But this was a shallow victory, for there was no singing and celebrating, no holding of hands, only the holding of turf. *Western Wall Story* has become a classic American Western, and Friday evening has become its *High Noon*.

And when I looked up, the dove was gone.

The *Shechina* has left the building.

And where has she gone? Why to the Mall, of course, where the people of Israel share a common language and meet on an equal canvas, bearing firstfruits and exchanging them for a sip of coffee and a snippet of intimate conversation. Everyone is there, sharing small talk at Sbarros on Jerusalem's Ben Yehuda Street, or folk dancing at Ben and Jerry's on Tel Aviv's beachfront.

If this all reeks of American cultural imperialism, I beg to differ. While the Western Wall has become bad Disney, the Mall has made Burger King a touchstone to the Sacred. A kosher Kentucky Fried Chicken isn't about the Americanization of Israel, it's about the Judaization of Americanism—at long last Colonel Sanders has discovered our secret recipe for the sanctification of life. At the new Jerusalem Mall there is equal access from every gate. Priests, Levites, women, the disabled, tourists: all are treated in like manner. A Mall with honest shop owners, separate meat and dairy food courts, and even a synagogue is a Mall that conveys the best of our value system to the next generation. Amid the Hebrew Coca-Cola bottles and Michael Jordan magazines is a level of holiness, because they are bringing my children and their Israeli cousins together in a Jewish state speaking a Jewish language.

The Mall, democratic, serendipitous, wide-eyed, infused with Jewish values, just a little bit dirty, and a whole lot Israeli, has become a place of pilgrimage and unity for the Jewish people—just what the Temple's outer courtyard used to be. The *Shechina* now sits on a nest of AstroTurf atop the Hard Rock Cafe, weeping no longer, for her people have returned. But alas, how lonely sit the ancient stones of the Kotel. I weep for them.

Mensch•Mark 32

WHERE SPRING
FOREVER DWELLS

Discovering That the
Promised Land Is Right Here

The great poet of early Zionism longed, as we all long, for a place where his people could find harmony and peace together. So do I. And I found it.

I've been thinking a lot about Bialik's bird lately. The great poet laureate of early Zionism, Hayyim Nachman Bialik, called his first published poem *"El ha-Tzipor"* ("To the Bird") when he composed it in 1892 in frigid Russia. It was as much a part of my childhood Hebrew school curriculum as the Ten Commandments. Here, in translation, is a selection from that sixteen-stanza classic:

> *Greetings! Peace to you, returning*
> *Lovely bird, unto my window*

From a warmer clime!
How my soul for songs was yearning
When my dwelling you deserted
In the wintertime.
. . . Do you bring me friendly greetings
From my brothers there in Zion,
Brothers far yet near?
O the happy! O the blessed!
Do they guess what heavy sorrows
I must suffer here?
Do my brothers know and could they picture
How many rise against me,
How their hatred swells?
Singing, singing O my birdling,
Sing of the wonders of the land where
Spring forever dwells.

Bialik was very young, just nineteen, when he wrote this. The depth of his torment resembles that of the two separated young lovers of the Song of Songs, his mood swinging furiously between the extremes of youthful passion and despair. The poet, envious of the bird's seasonal migrations to Zion, languishes in a bitter exile.

Times have certainly changed. Envy still exists, but for me it is more focused on the bard than the bird, for Bialik was able to yearn for Zion with an ardor that so few contemporary Jews express openly. I envy that passion. Meanwhile, that swelling hatred, once directed at Bialik's generation in Russia, now is focused primarily on those very brethren in the land of Israel whom the poet yearned to join.

If Bialik's bird could talk, it would tell us that spring still forever dwells in our troubled homeland and that we must reintensify our yearning for Zion. Even amid the bombs and mortar shells, the spring prevails.

And it would add something else, something Bialik could never have imagined.

From May to September, my congregation takes advantage of our synagogue's rustic surroundings and prays outdoors when weather permits. When we do, our chanting is augmented by a chorus of birds overhead, including those man-made ones departing from LaGuardia, Kennedy, and Newark, en route to Boston, Europe, and points east. And each week, like Bialik before me, I look up, marveling at what these migratory creatures might say if they could speak of their wondrous adventures.

When I was younger, I used to dream of being on those planes and flying to the most magical spots on earth, maybe even to Israel itself. In the cold northeast winters of my childhood, I imagined that each aircraft aloft, like Bialik's bird, was most certainly headed to a place filled with palm trees, exotic music, and eternal spring—and possibly Herve Villechaize shouting, "De plane! De plane!"

Then one gorgeous midsummer Shabbat eve a couple of years ago, as I was finishing the silent devotion with my congregants in the synagogue garden, I looked up, fixed my gaze upon a high-flying jet, and my perspective changed completely. Rather than speculating about it, I imagined a passenger on that plane looking down at us: a Jewish businessman headed to London to close a deal, sipping his Dewar's and missing his family, ungrounded, untethered to his past, and unaware that the Shabbat bride had just entered his air space.

So he looks down and sees a synagogue; he figures it's a synagogue because there is no cross and, hey, it's Friday night, and isn't that when Jews pray or something? And outside on the lawn there is a group of people, all ages, singing together.

He sees us swaying, in harmony with the rhythms of the week and the seasons, encircling one another while gazing both upward and eastward. He squints and sees children laughing, and thinks of his own kids, who are probably playing Nintendo at the moment, or screaming at the dog. He swallows hard, leans back in his chair, and wistfully recalls those pointless Bar Mitzvah lessons of his childhood, and a young adulthood sacrificed to the rat race, wondering how everything got so crazy.

Like Bialik, he longs for a Promised Land he never knew. He wishes, more than anything else, that he could be on the ground, with us.

This man on the plane is now a bird of *pray*, gazing in astonishment at the scene of serenity below. He intuits that Sartre was wrong, that, in fact, heaven—not hell—is other people. Like Balaam, the biblical Moabite prophet (sent not by Bialik but by Balak, the son of Tzipor, I might add), this outsider wishes so much to reject what he is looking at, but as he opens his mouth all he can do is echo the sweet song he is hearing in his mind's ear, "How delightful are your sanctuaries, O Israel." The bird sings.

There are people who have never heard of Hayyim Nachman Bialik, who yearn for grounding every bit as much as Bialik longed for flight. We must extend a hand and help them down from their perch. Whereas a century ago the bard was envious of the bird, the roles have now reversed. And where Bialik's Zionism was rooted in the need for a Jewish refuge in Israel, the most Zionist thing we can do now is to make the Jewish pulse beat more vibrantly right here and to lure back those who have long since taken flight from our synagogues and schools. They want to return—almost as much as they need to return—to us and then, with our help, to Zion.

They gaze at us from far above, from first class or coach, in their offices or at home, with their perpetual jet lag and their unfulfilled lives. Wherever they are, Bialik's new birds are listening closely for us to sing of the wonders of the land where spring forever dwells.

Mensch•Mark 33

KOSHER PIGS

Hypocrisy Can Be a Good Thing

The late and beloved Rabbi Richard Israel once wrote a book entitled *The Kosher Pig*. The intriguing title stems from a story he tells about a pious Jew who was told by his doctor that he had a rare disease that could be cured only by eating pork. Now Jewish law states that in order to save a life, virtually any of its requirements can—in fact, must—be broken. But that wasn't enough for this man. He determined that the pig had to be slaughtered in the kosher way, painlessly, before he ate it. So he brought the pig to the local ritual slaughterer, who acquired a special knife that would never be used on a kosher animal. After slaughtering it in the "proper" ritual manner, the *Shochet* examined the pig's lungs to look for blemishes. He had no idea what he was looking at, but he finally concluded that the lungs had no serious abrasions (and was therefore "smooth" or *glatt*).

"So, nu?" the man asked. "Rabbi, is this pig kosher?"

The rabbi examined the lungs for some time and then declared, "It may be kosher, but it's still a pig."

Modern Jewish life is filled with kosher pigs, utter inconsistencies that we sometimes hardly notice, but they are there, and they are enlightening.

This year, Passover begins on a Saturday night, something we haven't experienced since 1994. I can recall receiving numerous inquiries that year as to when one should stop eating bread: on Friday morning or Saturday morning? I tend to go by the book on matters of tradition (when I sneeze, I even say "Ah-choo!"), so without hesitation, I offered the traditional response, which is that the house should be virtually *hametz*-free (leaven-free) on Friday before Shabbat.

Now why is that?

Because one is not supposed to clean a house on Shabbat, or do the kinds of things we do to get rid of leaven: burn it, sell it, etc., the kinds of activities, incidentally, that most Jews would not hesitate to undertake on any given Shabbat.

To be "consistent" with his normal practice, the non-Shabbat observer should simply have ignored my advice and eaten bread until Saturday morning. Why should this Shabbat be different from all other Shabbats? That week in 1994, however, many people had their houses ready for Passover by Friday afternoon because they wanted to do Passover "right," when, in fact, they were rushing their preparations in order to keep Shabbat rules they don't normally keep.

The same thing happens every year regarding dietary restrictions. On Passover, otherwise non-*Kashrut*-observant Jews become fanatic about ridding their homes of leaven and bringing matzah sandwiches to the classroom or office. A ham-on-matzah sandwich is hardly an unthinkable scenario in this perplexing world of kosher pigs. It's kind of like the guy who drives to synagogue on Yom Kippur but tells the policeman writing him a ticket that he can't put money in the meter on a Jewish holiday.

A gem from Richard Israel's book: "Rabbi, I am marrying an Episcopalian woman. Can I get married during the week after Passover?"

And another: "An observant Jew has just made a serious pass at me. Do you think he will want me to go to Mikva [ritual bath] before I have an affair with him?"

Oy.

One commercial fisherman in California called his rabbi to see if it was kosher to use pieces of squid as bait when he goes fishing. An interesting question because squid has no fins and scales and is therefore unkosher, but does it affect the *Kashrut* of the fish caught? A fascinating question, except that he called the rabbi on Saturday morning to ask it.

Harold Kushner tells of another beaut. He was at a clergy meeting, and everyone brown-bagged their lunches. The local Reform rabbi brought a ham and cheese sandwich, and before he began to eat it, he paused and recited *ha-motzi*. His Orthodox colleague said to him, "Aren't you being a hypocrite, saying that prayer over blatantly non-kosher food?" He replied, "Not at all. The Jewish dietary laws don't impress me as religiously valuable, but the habit of thanking God for having food to eat impresses me very much."

Kushner's reaction is interesting. He disagrees with that rabbi's evaluation of the dietary laws, as do I, but he appreciates the seriousness of the response. A good Jew, he concludes, cannot be measured by checking someone's dietary habits or counting how often someone prays. A good Jew is someone who is constantly striving to become a better Jew.

All of these people are, to some degree, serious Jews, and for that alone we must commend them. We might laugh at the inconsistency, we might even call it hypocrisy, but if they are hypocrites, we should all be so hypocritical.

Webster's defines hypocrisy as being from the Greek for acting a part, pretending to be what one is not. And we know a hypocrite when we see one. As Adlai Stevenson once said of Richard Nixon, "He's the kind of politician who would cut down a redwood tree and then mount the stump to make a speech for conservation." That's hypocrisy, but we all must learn the difference between hypocrisy and inconsistency, between pretending and striving, between going halfway in earnest and throwing it all away without giving it half a chance.

You know, a little hypocrisy isn't so bad at times. It's not the worst sin to pretend a little, to play out what we may not fully believe. Sometimes, in fact, often, when I pray, I don't feel it; I certainly don't agree with every word. But I utter the words over and over again, and I help others to pray, and somehow, just because I've remained open to the prayers, a time does come when the words reveal worlds to me, and it all comes together. It happens. It really does. But for the person who says it's all or nothing, who refuses to pray because he thinks it means nothing to him and he doesn't want to be a hypocrite, the gates of wonder remain closed.

To be a hypocrite often means that at least you've set high, virtuous goals for yourself, even if you don't always live up to them. I'd rather do that and fall short than set no high standards at all. That's why religious leaders and politicians are so often called hypocrites while mobsters never are. Religious leaders have to ask us to aim high, while some people are forever stooping to reach their ideals. Most of us are so afraid of being called hypocrites that we take the easy road. If we expect little of ourselves, we usually deliver.

So as we approach this unusual alignment of Passover and Shabbat, let's allow for a little kosher pigheadedness. If you've rarely kept Shabbat in this manner before, don't feel funny about keeping it a little more meticulously this time. You might even enjoy it. It's okay to be inconsistent, especially when the alternative is to cop an all-or-nothing plea and then cop out.

PART SIX

Failure, Forgiveness, Justice, and Kindness

*. . . In which I confront lessons learned
from failure, including the need to forgive
myself and others. To err is human, after all.
But to forgive is human, too. In the end, we
return to those fundamental benchmarks
of being a mensch: the pursuit of justice
and the right of every human being to be
loved unconditionally.*

"How do you spell 'love'?" (Piglet)
"You don't spell it . . . you feel it." (Pooh)

—A. A. Milne, Winnie-the-Pooh

Love is the only sane and satisfactory answer
to the problem of human existence.

—Erich Fromm

For God's anger lasts a moment;
divine love is lifelong.

—Psalm 30

Mensch•Mark 34

2 0 1 1 , 2 0 1 2 , 2 0 1 8

CRISIS

My Greatest Test of Faith

In mid-December 2011, as adulation for the football star Tim Tebow was all the rage, I wrote an article that questioned the messianic faith espoused both by and toward the Broncos quarterback. I was drawing a connection between religious extremism and sports fanaticism at a time when the Tebow phenomenon had hit a fever pitch of almost unimaginable intensity. I wrote it during the week when his Broncos were set to face my team, the New England Patriots, in a game that would draw unprecedented interest, resulting in one of the highest TV ratings ever for a regular season contest. This followed a stretch of games where the evangelical football phenom had engineered a number of last-second victories that were being termed "miraculous." I was concerned that an increasing number of people were seeing divine intervention at work in the quarterback's heroics. As I pitched it to my editor, "If he wins the Super Bowl, it will be considered a real miracle [not just a football "miracle"]; his faith is so alluringly simplistic and powerful."

While I was working on the article, I saw an article *Slate* published entitled "Reality is now indistinguishable from fan fiction," featuring this tongue-in-cheek scenario that was in synch with my own thinking:

> I'm expecting to see Tebow get decapitated by James Harrison in the AFC Championship game, then rise from the dead as Madonna writhes across his tomb while lip-syncing "Like a Prayer" at the Super Bowl XLVI halftime show. The reanimated Tebow, brought on in favor of an ineffective Brady Quinn, will complete one pass for a loss of two yards, leading the Broncos to a comeback win over the previously undefeated Packers as Von Miller sacks Aaron Rodgers fourteen times and Ryan Grant runs untouched into the wrong end zone for a Denver safety as time expires. On ESPN's *First Take* the next morning, Skip Bayless and Merrill Hoge will debate whether Tebow is the risen Christ and if he needs to become more of a downfield passing threat for the Broncos to repeat.

SNL played on the same Tebow-as-savior theme in a skit the following weekend. It's hard, in retrospect, to overstate the fervor that ignited America that week. Even when Red Sox fans were experiencing their Curse Reversal in 2004, the messianic feelings transcended any one religious group while Tebow mania was completely intertwined with Christian fundamentalism. Many were certain that this man was God's Chosen Quarterback, their faith unflinching.

I've always felt that faith, real faith, the kind that Jesus, Moses, and Mohammed modeled, must, in fact, *be* flinching, anchored not by certainty but by the constant challenges of doubt. I subscribe to the philosophy of Paul Tillich, who said "Doubt isn't the opposite of faith; it is an element of faith." So I tried to convey my concerns in an article that, while projecting a serious message, I'd also written using the tongue-in-cheek manner that has long been my signature style (if you've read this far in this book, I think you know that), employing some phraseology that I would later call, in the greatest understatement of my career, "un-artful."

A better word would have been *dumb*.

Actually. The word *hateful* might not be that far off.

I played with the notion that if we were seeing such fervor during the regular season, and given the kind of rioting so often seen following championship games (as evidenced just a few months before, following the Stanley Cup final in Vancouver), it was unimaginable what a Broncos Super Bowl victory would bring. And then I proceeded to imagine it: a landscape of unleashed fury that would involve potential hate crimes. I suggested that Tebow's emboldened followers could do "insane things, like burning mosques, bashing gays and indiscriminately banishing immigrants."

Some people didn't find it funny.

In fact, lots of people didn't.

Let's be clear. Apparently, millions of people didn't.

In fact, looking back at it, I don't either. It was one of my few major journalistic blunders, but it was no mere slipup.

What I had done was to step on not one but two "third rails" of American life simultaneously, sports and religion, and in doing so I had simultaneously stepped on a third, election year politics. It was the beginning of a contentious presidential election cycle, one in which morality and religion were to figure highly, where social media feeding frenzies would take down even the most experienced pundits. No sooner than the media caravan moved on from me did they revel in the misstatements of Rush Limbaugh's calling Sandra Fluke a "slut" and "prostitute," CNN's Roland Martin for anti-gay tweets at the Super Bowl, and CNN's Hilary Rosen's controversial comments about stay-at-home moms.

What separated my comments from theirs was that my day job is to be the representative of an entire congregation—and by extension the Jewish people—and, to a degree, God—before humanity. Cable pundits are expected to make controversial comments; even in the *gotcha* world that social media has spawned, their margin for error was far greater than mine.

More context: On December 7, just before I wrote the article, a group of *Jewish* extremists set fire to a mosque on the West Bank. It was one of a series of what have been dubbed "Price Tag" attacks primarily on mosques but also on Christian religious sites. Add to that the Koran burning by Florida Pastor Terry Jones, an evangelical, earlier that year. In 2011, according to FBI statistics, the number of bias crimes against the LGBTQ community was even greater than those directed against people because of their religion.

These incidents angered me. So I wasn't writing specifically about evangelicals, Christians, or sports fans, and certainly not the people of Denver. I was bemoaning a culture of increasing violence and extremism on all fronts. But I wasn't clear enough about that and mishmashed it all together.

I was seething at the horrors people had done in God's name, so I threw the journalistic equivalent of a Hail Mary, hoping to diffuse the extremism I saw brewing around me among people of many faith traditions, not just Christians. My article was intended to be a stark warning about the dangers of unwavering certainty and the resultant intolerance, and yet now I was being accused of precisely that sin, of intolerance—and for good reason. My sarcasm had only served to exacerbate the national divide.

To explain is not to excuse. There is no excuse. I am not justifying anything I wrote. Even as I look back at this from the perspective of late 2018, with all the cruelty that has been perpetrated upon Syrian refugees and Central American asylum seekers, including the forced separation of children from parents, I still can not justify what I wrote. There is no "I told you so" to be had here. I went too far. It is wrong to paint an entire group of people with so broad an accusatory brush, as I had done. The way to combat hate is not with more acrimony but with more love. Constructive criticism goes much further than rank sarcasm. My job is to be part of the solution, not to exacerbate the problem.

I grasped that things were getting out of hand a day after the article was published online. It was all about that one line, so I agreed with my editor that the offensive line should be removed and I immediately called my synagogue president to apprise him of the situation. But it was already too late. I realized this when a producer for Sean Hannity called me and asked for an interview, which I politely declined. Before I knew it, I was being slammed on several Fox News programs, and then it spread to other media outlets. I chose not to fan the flames with a more detailed response and turned down more offers to defend myself on national television and in the press. It was a wise choice. I began to get calls from concerned congregants and other friends. One congregant even called to say congratulations; he had seen my picture on *The Five* while walking on the treadmill at the gym, with the volume turned off.

Angry responses to my article began to go viral in the blogosphere. It was my fifteen minutes of shame. If you do an online search of my name (and many months passed before I could), you will still see that a significant chunk of the internet defined me as a bigoted, small-minded Christian hater. I received hundreds of hate emails, a few of them constructive, all of them painful. Among the anonymous comments left on my blog were anti-Semitic statements so shocking and vile that I couldn't even bring myself to report them—especially after hearing that the ADL was also considering publicly condemning me. After seeing many of these anonymous postings, I turned off the comments option to my blog. I haven't turned it back on since.

Here's one of the anonymous comments:

After reading your bullshit, I find it amusing that to this day, jews still can't comprehend why the world hates you. Look in the mirror, or simply read your bullshit to someone with a brain! We won't miss you next time!

Imagine. I had spent my entire life building bridges between groups, trying to show Judaism in its best light, as a religion of love, and now I found myself looking at what could be construed as a death threat. *And I couldn't even share it with the Anti-Defamation League*, fearful that they would just tell me that I deserved it.

I got the name of a top-notch LA damage control consultant, and we carefully crafted an apology, which we sent out the next day. I let it stand as the only public comment I would make about the matter for many months. The apology appeared all over the mainstream media, but it did little to stem the tide of anger. Everyone just assumed I was a hater. I began to wonder if perhaps I was.

Looking back at what I wrote and how poorly I conveyed my thoughts, I really blew it. But had I really set back the cause of the Jewish people? Had I done something more vile and less forgivable than the pastor who burned a Koran? Was I now on that level? And, when weighed against my entire career, was this fair?

Was there a way out of this?

What followed was the most severe test of faith I've faced in a rabbinic career that, to that point, had spanned a quarter of a century. The ensuing days nearly ruined me. A professional and personal reputation carefully crafted over the course of decades appeared to have come crashing down. I was derided by rabbinic colleagues, friends, relatives, and strangers alike. Those who stood by me did so out of pure loyalty or pity, but even many of them took great pains to dissociate themselves from my words. Jews accused me of giving anti-Semites license to hate, and, judging from my inbox, I couldn't disagree. But deep down I understood that although the words may have been narrow-minded, the person who wrote them is not. I clung to that belief as the hurricane around me intensified.

I fled from the same social media and news outlets that had been my lifeblood, unable to bear the pain of reading more comments, each menacing subject line a new dagger. But every few seconds I would hear the "ping" of a new Google alerts email, indicating that my name had just been mentioned somewhere Out There. These pings sounded like the drip, drip, drip, *beeeep* of a hospital room, with the IV bag containing my ebbing reputation, as I sat alongside my basement computer for hours, powerless to do anything but listen and delete, listen and delete, listen and delete.

My usual avenue of escape, sports, was not available to me. I turned on *Inside the NFL* to hear Chris Collinsworth pillory those spewing hate against Tebow (thankfully not naming me, though I recall his mentioning something about "religious leaders"). I watch the Sunday news shows religiously. But not that week, because they took their shot at me, too.

Finally, there was the Broncos-Patriots game, which, had the Broncos won, would only have amped up Tebow mania even more and intensified the outcry. In the second quarter, the Broncos had a significant lead. Despairing, I called my closest friend while my eyes remained glued to the game, wondering how low this could this go. But the Patriots rallied, led somewhat improbably by Aaron Hernandez, a college teammate of Tebow's who would be arrested for murder several months later. On this day, the murderer beat the messiah and saved the rabbi. The Lord works in mysterious ways. I've never enjoyed a Patriots victory less. And I've never needed one more.

Over those difficult days, when I dared to venture forth from my basement office, I assumed that every person on the street was staring at me with scorn. I looked into the gaze of total strangers, guessing whether that person "knew." I counseled myself the way I've counseled so many others over the years, reminding myself, mantra-like, "It gets better." It could not have gotten much worse. I felt for my kids, who had to deal with this everywhere they went. It wasn't the first time that my job had affected their lives, but this was far more intense than any previous challenge. Never before had they had to field hate messages off our answering machine. My family was incredibly, unbelievably supportive when I needed them most.

Our society is filled with stories of clergy falling from grace, but in most cases they succumb to temptations of greed or lust and ruin the lives of victims and followers. All I had done was write one questionable sentence, a few ill-chosen words among the millions of insightful, inspiring, and occasionally life-changing words I have written over the years, and yet my name was being disparaged as if I'd robbed the collection plate. Even my scandals are boring! I lamented at the unfairness but did not respond. In fact, I stopped writing altogether for several months, which for me is like quitting breathing, cold (vegetarian) turkey.

The congregation was enormously supportive, with very few exceptions. Many considered the matter overblown, but even if they had concerns, since they knew who I really was, they weren't buying the media portrayal of bigotry personified.

My spirits were buoyed by the local interfaith council of which I had been president and have always been a champion of interfaith dialogue. The board, consisting of Christians, Jews, Muslims, and others, and led by Rev. Kate Heichler, sent the local newspaper a statement. Their response laid, for me, the seeds of salvation:

> To the editor:
> We have been distressed to read the recent letters here about Rabbi Joshua Hammerman and his "Tebow" column. He admitted himself that he did not communicate well, and his attempt at

hyperbole went too far. But we imagine we've all written or said something which we regret (often posted on the internet for eternity) and we shudder to think of anyone who has written so many excellent columns being judged by one that misfired.

We object to seeing a valued friend and colleague smeared as prejudiced when he has been more active in engaging interfaith conversation and education than most. As Pastor Tommie Jackson said, "He does not have a vicious or bigoted bone in his body."

We think the vast majority of his congregants would agree. Rabbi Hammerman is a past president of the Interfaith Council, the first pulpit rabbi to hold that position.

In a healthy community, people can talk about matters of conflict without invective. In a healthy community, people see one another in the context of their whole lives, not by one misguided statement. In a healthy community—especially in communities of faith—people treat one another with mercy and truth and the kind of love that transforms us into the people we can be. We hope those attacking Rabbi Hammerman in these pages and elsewhere might remember when their missteps have been greeted with mercy, and practice this kind of love.

I cried when I read that statement. Never had I felt so touched by God's love, and it came at a time when I had never felt so alone.

Gradually, life returned to normal—the new normal, a normal in which I scrutinized even more carefully every word I composed. A world in which I set aside grand literary projects for more immediate ones and prayed, quietly, for Tim Tebow to lose a few more games. When the Patriots knocked him from the playoffs, I exhaled, and my pen stayed still.

I did write to Tebow a sincere apology, along with a humble request for a more substantive dialogue. I wanted to learn more about his faith.

A few days later, I received a form letter from his foundation. I would still love to hear from him. I think there is much we could learn from each other.

Then ten months after the original article was published, on Yom Kippur, I stood before over 1,500 fellow sufferers and for the first time spoke in public about the ordeal. That sermon helped me to move on.

As I sat down to write, the question was, what kind of sermon would it be?

I could have spoken about the unfairness. I could have focused on the evils of intolerance and extremism, as I had attempted to do in the article. I could have focused on the deep depression that had engulfed me.

But I chose instead to speak about failure. It was the right choice. By turning my comeuppance into a universal lesson, I helped many of those present to confront their own failings. I helped many sitting in the congregation to forgive those who had let them down (including, I suppose, me). I know of some who were coaxed back from the edge of despair, helped to understand that it does get better. I'll never know how many I helped, but I do know that a snarky, defensive rebuttal to Sean Hannity on that horrible December day would have accomplished none of the above.

That sermon enabled the congregation to achieve a needed closure nearly a year after the original Tebow article. The scars remained, both in my psyche and on my Google page. Resentments still bubble within me not too far from the surface. I wonder how I could have been so careless, and how others, people who know me, could have interpreted my words so maliciously. I wonder how different it would have been if I had not been a rabbi, and, like so many pundits who embrace controversy for whom there is no such thing as bad publicity, I had greater margin for error.

But on that Yom Kippur of 2012, I stood bare and unmasked before the community. A rabbi is a professional human being, after all. It's my job to model imperfection, repentance, and return. Experiencing this episode of failure allowed me to do my job better than I ever had before. And it was the kind of sermon that would have been much more difficult to deliver in the first half of my career.

Time has passed and the world is a very different place. The worlds of cable news and social media have become exponentially more vicious and unforgiving (I can only imagine what Russian bots would have done with me). I'm writing again with confidence, though editing more carefully, and Tim Tebow has become yesterday's messiah, for the moment.

God has taken both Tim Tebow and me on a long, tortuous path. My voyage is far less glamorous but no less instructive. I've learned much about how to carve out a life of meaning and dignity in a digital era that can turn one's existence overnight into an instant hell.

I've grown to better understand the machinations of faith and forgiveness and have come to embrace the virtues of failure.

As a postscript, I wrote to Tebow again a couple of years later, again asking him whether he might want to engage in a dialogue that might enable people to better understand our different religious perspectives. I received a nice autographed postcard from his foundation in return.

As I delivered one of the most important sermons of my life, one meant exclusively for my congregants and was never shared in print or online, I fell back on an old adage.

To err is human.

It's a lesson the human rabbi had to learn the hard way.

So now, for the first time in print, I share that sermon.

2012 Yom Kippur

Last December I wrote an article that began to circulate in the blogosphere and then, after being picked up by Fox News, went viral.

You may have heard about it. It caused somewhat of a stir. It was my fifteen minutes of shame. Although local response was much more muted, the article caused embarrassment to at least some of you, and until now I have not had the chance to personally apologize. I expressed my feelings to the board personally and circulated a written statement. But given the charged political climate, which in our society has pretty much eliminated the potential for reasoned discourse, I chose not to fan the flames with a more detailed response and turned down several offers to defend myself on national television and in the press.

It was a failure—my failure—a failure to communicate, primarily, to communicate my ideas properly. Not a moral failing or character flaw, as some tried to portray it, though those stinging accusations caused me to place a large mirror in front of my face; but in my line of work, a communication failure is no small thing. I take responsibility for every word I write and speak—there have literally been millions of those words since I came here twenty-five years ago—and I know that everything that I say or write not only represents me but also you to some extent and, to a degree, the entire Jewish people.

That's what it's like to be a rabbi. Every word counts. And this is the right time and place for me to apologize to you, to clean up this bit of unfinished business as we move forward together into the New Year.

I am humbled by the fact that the local community was so supportive. Beth El's leadership acted responsibly and sensitively. And the reaction of my fellow clergy from the interfaith council, and in particular the letter they wrote defending me, was perhaps the moment in my life when I felt most directly touched by God's love. I am grateful to them and to all of you.

The full story of what happened last winter will have to wait for another day. In fact, the intended message of that article was precisely the point I made last week on the first day of Rosh Hashanah when I said: "There are those who seek to use religion as a lever to divide us rather than as a banner to unite us. But religion has a role to play, a very important role, in a world of upheaval. It can help to bring people together." I said it much better last week than I did last December.

Today, though, I don't want to dwell on the question of religious extremism. Today I'd like to jump off from this to focus on a more appropriate topic for Yom Kippur: failure itself.

I've learned quite a bit this year about the nature of failure in our "gotcha" society and how important it is to get back up and not be afraid to risk falling again.

In this unforgiving environment, especially in an election year, it's not just rabbis who face added scrutiny. Candidates certainly do, and we see almost daily examples of words being twisted or taken out of context. No good phrase goes unpunished. And when they clearly misspeak, no admission of failure is tolerated. It's considered a sign of weakness, when, in fact, most of us would consider it refreshingly honest.

This is where the world is right now. Our country is now more polarized than at any time since the Civil War, and in an age of 24/7 news coverage, whatever people say can and will be used against them, even if they said it eons ago. The list is endless of people whose misstatements have fed the partisan, political body-slam machine.

Some pundits, on the left and the right, deliberately try to be provocative, and when they really cross the line—we've seen a few horrible examples of that this year—they issue pseudo-remorseful clarifications for political expediency, and then a week later they are right back at it. But most failures aren't deliberate; they are simply slips of the tongue or on-the-spot miscalculations.

Why can't we just relax and recognize that people make mistakes? It's okay to make them, and it's okay to confess to them, and it's okay to forgive them. Clint Eastwood talked to an empty chair. No big deal . . . I speak to empty seats all the time!

Which reminds me of a joke. Two men were watching a John Wayne movie and one said to the other, "I'll bet you a dollar that John Wayne falls off a horse within five minutes." The other man accepted the bet and within five minutes, John Wayne fell off the horse.

The man wanted to pay, but the first man refused saying, "I saw the film already and can't accept your money." The second man replied, "I saw it, too."

"Then why did you accept the bet?"

"I didn't think John Wayne would be foolish enough to make the same mistake twice."

No one is too big to fail. Not even John Wayne. Some corporations might be too big to fail. Some banks might be. Some auto manufacturers might be. But that's what makes them different from human beings. *No person is too big to fail.*

Failure is not an option . . . it's a given. It is inevitable. We're all going to fail at some point. Moses did. King David did, big time. Murder, theft, and adultery: the trifecta, and his lust-driven crime inspired some of the liturgy of the *Sh'ma Kolenu* prayer. We all fail.

Heck, even God fails. Back to that midrash that I've been quoting this week: imagine, God created and destroyed the world several times over before hitting upon the right combination. In chapter six of Genesis, God even expresses regret for having created human beings. Commentators are aghast that a supposedly omnipotent God could feel that way. But the verse is right there, right before the story of Noah and the flood. It's hard to ignore.

"The Lord *regretted* making the man—God was heartbroken over it." What's that all about?

We can find a clue in the only other usage of that expression "*Vaynachem Adonai*" in the Torah. It's in Exodus 32:

"And the Lord *repented of the evil* which God had spoken of doing to God's people."

It's the golden calf incident, and Moses convinces God not to destroy Israel. In the case of the flood, God regrets having created humanity, destroys everything, and starts again. In the case of the golden calf, God regrets *wanting* to destroy, has mercy toward the people, and steps back from the precipice.

A blogger called "The Curious Jew" points out the "great distinction between 'Flood Logic' and 'Golden Calf Logic.' 'Flood Logic' assumes that the world must be perfect, and that wickedness cannot be tolerated. (There the God of Justice reigns) . . . In 'Golden Calf Logic,' it is the God of Mercy who is dominant, God who understands the flaws and who is able to tolerate wickedness, comprehending that these errors can be rectified."

Interesting. It's almost as if God undergoes a process of growth in the Torah, something that is, by the way, very consistent with how the ancients viewed God. The lesson here is not to expect perfection. By the time we get to the golden calf, which, as failures go, was a doozy, God has learned that no one is too big to fail.

God has learned it.

And the word *Vayinachem,* which here means "repented," can also mean "was comforted." In that translation, the verse from Genesis could be read, "And God was *comforted* at having created humanity—though also disheartened." The comfort could come from the knowledge that although the experiment looked like a failure, God recognized that this human being would be a resilient creature. Yes, things were going to get hairy. Moses would hit the rock and David would hit rock bottom, but in the end it would be okay.

Failure is not an option. It's a given.

So how do we deal with our own shortcomings?

The Yom Kippur liturgy is all about responding to failure. The Kol Nidre prayer is a perfect example. All the oaths, vows, and promises that we could not fulfill . . . well, they're annulled! Done! We get a mulligan! We tried our best. It's okay! We know we'll do better next time. Can't stop making promises even if we can't fulfill them all. But we can't give up trying. And this afternoon we read the book of Jonah, a story where everyone messes up, and everyone gets a second chance. We'll be taking a closer look at that book during our break, for those who wish to stay around.

In Silicon Valley, they call failure the "F word" that entrepreneurs say all the time. For every high-tech business success, there are countless failures, but there failure is accepted, or even welcomed, as a guide for future success. One investing partner at Google Ventures said, "In my mind, the ones who have no fear of failure are merely the dreamers, and the dreamers don't build great companies."

Everywhere you look these days, outside of politics and the media, that is, people are extolling the virtues of failure. And if ever you want to read about the desirability and inevitability of failure, look no further than commencement addresses.

Aaron Sorkin told graduates at Syracuse this year, "To get where you're going, you have to be good . . . Every once in a while, you'll succeed. Most of the time you'll fail, and most of the time the circumstances will be well beyond your control."

Sounds like an episode of *everything Aaron Sorkin's ever written.*

Steve Carell told graduates at Princeton this year, "When I was in college, I wouldn't 'text' a girl to ask her out on a date. I would ask her, in person. One human being to another. And when she said no, which she always did, I would suffer the humiliation and self-loathing that a young man needs for his, or her, personal growth."

Newark Mayor Cory Booker, at Bard: "I believe in my heart of hearts that it is better to have your ship sunk at sea than have it rot in the harbor."

Love it! Though I would prefer a third option.

And Atul Gawande, the physician and author, said at Williams

College that what great hospitals prove to be really great *at* was rescuing people when they have a complication, preventing failures from becoming catastrophes.... "They call them a 'Failure to Rescue.' More than anything, this is what distinguishes the great from the mediocre. They don't fail *less*. They rescue *more*."

He makes failure sound like a good thing. And it is.

One of our teens spoke of failure in a valedictory speech at his middle school graduation last June. We need to be motivated by our failures, he said. We can't all get the same trophy.

So how can we take failure and grow from it?

First, we learn to accept it and embrace it.

A few weeks ago I was talking to a congregant, and the subject turned to his extraordinary father of blessed memory, a salesman extraordinaire, who forty years ago wrote a book that is seen by many as a salesman's bible. It has had several versions, one called *The 36 Biggest Mistakes Salesmen Make*. There are lots of mistakes listed there, everything from "Running with the pack" to "Giving up too quickly" to "Coming back with the same old pitch." But what does he put as the number one mistake salesmen make?

Rationalizing away your failures.

It's okay to fail, he states. It's *not* okay to shirk responsibility for it. You can come up with every excuse in the book, but you'll never grow from it unless you own it.

Another way we can grow from our failures is to help others deal with their failures. Again, this doesn't work in the intolerant, cutthroat areas of life, like politics, journalism, sports, business, academia, social media, locker room gossip, or, come to think of it, just about everywhere.

But let's try harder. Everyone deserves a second chance, something illustrated by this story:

A woman was at work when she received a phone call that her small daughter was very sick with a fever. She left work and stopped by the pharmacy to get some medication. She got back to her car and found that she had locked her keys in the car. She didn't know what to do. She called home and the babysitter told her that the fever was getting worse. She said: "You might find a coat hanger and use that to open the door."

The woman looked around and found an old rusty coat hanger that had been left on the ground, possibly by someone else who at some time had locked their keys in their car. But she had no idea how to use it, so she bowed her head and asked God to send help.

Within five minutes a beat-up old motorcycle pulled up. [On it rode a] bearded man who was wearing an old biker skull rag on his head.

The woman thought: "This is what you sent to help me?"

However, she was desperate. The man got off of his cycle and asked if he could help.

She said: "Yes, my daughter is very sick and I've locked my keys in my car. Please, can you use this hanger to unlock my car?"

He said "Sure." He walked over to the car, and in less than a minute the car was opened.

She hugged the man and through her tears she said "Thank you so much! You are a very nice man."

The man replied, "Lady, you probably should know that I just got out of prison yesterday. I was in prison for car theft."

The woman hugged the man again and with sobbing tears cried out loud "Oh, thank you, God! You even sent me a professional!!"

Yesterday's car thief can be today's Good Samaritan. Everyone deserves a second chance.

A third strategy for dealing with failure is to drown it in success.

Rabbi Joseph Telushkin tells the story of how his grandfather interpreted the verse from Psalm 34 "*Sur may'ra v'aseh tov*," "turn from evil and do good." He said that if one is given water filled with salt to drink, you have two choices. You can either desalinate the water—very expensive and not practical. Or you can add so much fresh water that the salt will become virtually unnoticeable.

The same goes with failure. You can waste your time being aggravated about something that can never be changed or undone, or you can instead do so many acts of kindness that eventually will overwhelm the earlier wrongful acts and make them seem much less significant.

When I was accused of having antipathy toward conservative evangelicals, I made it my business to try to understand them better and to reaffirm the centrality of interfaith dialogue in our work here. At AIPAC, I went to a session led by some evangelical leaders and established a correspondence with one of them. It's been helpful. I got to share some of my concerns about campus proselytizing and end time prophecies regarding Israel. I now have a better understanding of how such matters do not need to interfere with our mutual support of Israel. But efforts at dialogue won't stop there.

A local Muslim representative will speak here at a Shabbat service in January. Many of us are guilty of lumping people into groups. And in December, we'll be hearing from an award-winning filmmaker and author who will tell us about her friend, a Palestinian from the Old City of Jerusalem who has spent the last two decades working for peace. We need to be the congregation that brings groups together, and, given my experiences this year, I'm more determined than ever to do that.

In whatever way we feel we've fallen short of the mark, we can overwhelm the bad with good.

Incidentally, if you feel you need to overwhelm your sins with goodness, overwhelm us with your presence at Shabbat services. That's my prescription: Take two *minyans* and call me in the morning.

We also need to acknowledge that life is difficult.

As M. Scott Peck has written, once we truly know that life is difficult, then we can transcend it. Once it is accepted, the fact that life is difficult no longer matters. It becomes a given, a baseline. And understanding the messiness of life helps us to forgive our own imperfections and those of our neighbors.

But despite the obstacles, we mustn't play it safe.

Elie Wiesel said famously that the opposite of good is not evil but indifference. Similarly, I believe that the opposite of life is not death but *irrelevance*. The opposite of life is *purposeless life*, a life that was never really lived.

Now it's possible to be relevant in destructive ways, so one's life must also be guided by humility and kindness, what we Jews call *menschlichkeit*. But we can't fear risking failure, because even if we opt for the path of least resistance, failure will still happen.

It's easy to doubt yourself when confronted by failure, as I did. It is easy to wonder whether a lifetime of good work can be wiped away in an instant. It is easy to deflect blame and stoke up internal anger. It is easy to lose sleep. I did all of the above. I waited for everyone else to lift me up when I needed to do that myself.

And in the end, I realized that only I can define my legacy. Not Twitter, not my Facebook profile, not Google, and not even Fox News or MSNBC, for that matter. Our legacy is in our hands, and much of how we will be remembered has to do with how we rise when we have fallen short.

When Aly Raisman was warming up for the floor exercise in the women's team gymnastic finals at the recent Olympics, a blogger named Matthew Hunt noticed that she was showing a couple of big misses in her routine, causing the announcers to question whether she was ready for a gold medal performance. Of course she was, and that's why she is now our hero (for being so irrepressible, as well as being so proud of her heritage that she did her floor exercise to "Hava Nagila)." He speculated that she might have been falling on purpose. "Was she practicing failure in front of an audience?" Hunt wondered. "Making errors during warm up practice seems like exactly the right time to get the 'failures' out of the way."

It's like that 2006 Nike commercial with Michael Jordan. The commercial opens with a scene of Michael getting out of his limo and walking into the arena. While walking through the tunnel he is shaking hands and giving nods to the security and maintenance staff. The voiceover begins with him recognizing that he has missed over nine thousand shots in his career and lost almost three hundred games, and twenty-six times he has been trusted to take the game winning shot . . . and missed. The commercial ends with Michael walking through doors into the Players Entrance and finishes with his insight: "I have failed over, and over, and over again in my life . . . and *that* is why I succeed."

On Yom Kippur, we're not just talking about sinking jump shots and sticking the landing. We're exclaiming, "We've betrayed; we've stolen; we've become violent; we've caused others to do evil; we've lied; we've scoffed; we've rebelled; we've been scornful, stiff-necked, and corrupt." Serious stuff.

So pick your failure today. You don't have to be proud of it. You only need to grow from it. For no one is too big to fail. As we'll read next week on Sukkot in the book of Ecclesiastes (7:20), which basically says, "There is no person so perfectly righteous that he does only good and doesn't mess up."

The Kotzker Rebbe says, "The main element of sin is not how a person has sinned, for he is only human, and he could not withstand the test. The main element of sin is that a person may repent at any moment, but does not. And *this* sin is greater than the transgression itself." As we've learned time and time again in our society, the cover-up is always worse than the crime.

We've failed. But in our failure lies the seeds of forgiveness and, ultimately, salvation. Nachman of Bratzlav taught, "In the very obstacle that blocks you from discovering God is precisely where God is waiting to be discovered."

And a God who also models forgiveness.

If God could bear the imperfections of Abraham, Moses, Aaron, Jacob, Sarah, Miriam, and David, so must we forgive our own and those of others. And may we and those dear to us be granted a year of personal fulfillment, good health, spiritual growth, intensified connection with the Jewish people and the community, and the simple joy of being alive, today and every day.

Mensch•Mark 35

CHAMPIONING CIVILITY

It's Impossible to Avoid Gossip but Essential to Try

Civility has long been a prime concern of mine. Many Jews say to me, "Rabbi, I feel like I am a good person, even though I'm not a good Jew." Since when must the two be mutually exclusive? Jewish ritual is vacuous if it does not lead to ethical ends. Judaism, which should instinctively be linked to kindness, modesty, and honesty, too often is associated with ritual correctness, ethnic tribalism, and an unyielding ethic of holier-than-thou. "Nice" needs to be the Next Big Thing. When our communities project an ethos of love, generosity of spirit, humility, and acceptance, the world will notice. Words matter. As Jewish activist Nigel Savage wrote after the Tree of Life massacre in Pittsburgh in 2018, the fault line now is "between those who strive to use language with honesty and empathy and a desire to make things better; and those who use language to inflame, incite, exaggerate and demonize... our tree of life has taught us these two millennia—that language, and respectful discourse and truth are utterly central to being Jewish."

I wrote the following essay in the mid '90s, a much quainter time, when everyone in Washington got along ... except for that little impeachment thing.

What has become of civility?

We see its demise in Washington, where angry ideologues have driven the moderates underground; on talk shows, where hard-earned reputations are routinely demolished; from Giants Stadium, where catcalls led to iceballs, to our own offices, schools, and homes.

So I decided to launch a counterattack by being extraordinarily nice for a single day.

My inspiration came from Rabbi Joseph Telushkin, who originated the idea of a day when all Americans would refrain from hurtful speech. His book *Words That Hurt, Words That Heal* inspired Senators Joseph Lieberman and Connie Mack to table Senate Resolution #151, establishing a National Speak No Evil Day, calling on Americans to go a full day (May 14) without saying anything unkind or unfair about, or to, anyone.

I elected to go cold turkey on destructive language for twenty-four hours. These were my ground rules: 1) no cursing or screaming; 2) no negative statements about any third party not present; 3) utter courtesy in all interactions; and 4) no telling anyone about this little experiment.

I began at five o'clock on a Monday afternoon.

5:30 PM: My mother calls, giving me oodles of advice about relatives, the kids, work, health. By 5:45, she's broken me, and I revert to my usual role as the annoyed son and willing gossip partner. On both counts, I've blown it. I decide to call off my quest until midnight.

1:10 AM: Mara plops two-year-old Daniel next to me in bed, jarring me from dreams of making the world better for nice people. "I'm sorry, I didn't hear his screaming," I mutter. "I'll listen better next time." Perfect. I manage to suppress my knee-jerk response ("Listen, if the kid's bawling, why should we both have to suffer?") and defuse a potential chain reaction of verbal violence. I'm getting the hang of this.

5:05 AM: Four-year-old Ethan plows into the bed, screaming, "Daniel is in my spot!" Again, I subdue the anger impulse, suggesting calmly that all Hammerman children return to their own beds.

"Then carry me," my forty-nine-pound eldest demands, always able to sense weakness in his parental prey. I do, with a forced smile, like a senator making nice to a wealthy lobbyist.

7:30 AM: I tiptoe out the door, leaving the domestic part of my personal Speak No Evil Day successfully behind me.

As a rabbi, I represent a tradition that recognizes evil speech as an addiction and equates it with physical assault. But I'm human, too, and since I spend most of my day communicating, the potential for verbal lapse is ever-present. On this day, I need to avoid all temptation. Driving to my rounds at the hospital, I switch from Imus and Stern to classical music. I miss the dirt.

I need coffee.

9:25 AM: An elderly patient whispers to me that the hospital is filled with anti-Semites conspiring to steal her flowers. I hold her hand, calmly saying, "The people here are very nice." The word *nice* is beginning to get to me. As I leave the hospital, I smile at everyone, including an orderly sweeping the floor. He seems agitated. I'm stepping on his mop.

11:30 AM: Back at the office, I receive a phone call from a man moving to the 'burbs from Manhattan. I try to talk up Stamford without saying anything derogatory about the noisy, filthy, crime-infested city he inhabits (just kidding, Big Apple-ites; I love New York). It's not easy. I'm famished.

12:14 PM: As I return from a quick bite of anything-sweet-I-can-find, my secretary tells me that she didn't know I would be back so soon, so my 12:15 appointment, a potential new congregant, has left.

"You sent her *home*?!"

It's not quite a shout, but I know instantly that I've gone beyond my strict boundaries. I apologize profusely. It turns out the appointment is waiting for me in the library. She badmouths another local congregation. I go out of my way to defend it. The conversation fizzles after that.

With each encounter that follows, I walk on verbal eggshells. I meet with a divorced couple planning their child's Bar Mitzvah. Thankfully, both are there, so neither can talk about the other.

A close friend calls, a primary source for community gossip. I'm afraid to ask a simple "How is everything?" for fear of what could follow. I have a deep thirst for some juicy stuff and sense an unnatural distance between us. What can I say to convey warmth without it being at the expense of innocent others? The call ends, abruptly.

A congregant stops by to discuss a program she is working on and states flatly of a coworker, "Doesn't she drive you crazy?" Either a no or a yes makes me an accomplice to defamation. I pretend not to hear.

Another rabbi calls, asking me for an evaluation of a teacher applying for a job in his synagogue. I've only good things to say, but every word feels like a dagger, every sentence a thrust. Throughout the day, I manage to deflect deprecatory comments about everyone from the Lubavitcher Rebbe to Yasser Arafat.

3:30 PM: I am courteous to a phone solicitor offering "Rabie" Hammerman a Visa Gold card.

3:40 PM: I stand before seventy-five restless Hebrew school students, wishing to dock them from life eternal if they don't shut up. I've a splitting headache. I'm ready to give myself over to a higher power.

Exhausted, I go home, flick on the tube, and hear Dole attacking Forbes. I turn it off. In local news, Ethan reports that Daniel was pinching and kicking at gymnastics class. From day one we are pro-grammed to blame and defame.

The morning after: I am humbled by my noble failure and far less inclined to blame talk show hosts and Washingtonians for this national addiction. With or without a Senate resolution, I will have to shake it alone, step-by-step, word-by-word. On May 14, I'll try again.

Mensch•Mark 36

2011

"DO YOU THINK I'M EVIL?"

The Stain of Hatred on the Human Soul

A trip to South Africa moved me profoundly; particularly an encounter on a plane. The disease of racism is not a South African invention, and it has hardly been eradicated.

During a visit to South Africa last summer, I stopped at the Apartheid Museum in Johannesburg, hoping to better understand how so despicable a system could dominate that country for nearly half a century, from 1948 to 1991, and why any comparisons to Israel are ridiculous. I came away humbled, wondering whether a little residue of apartheid might be in us all.

After visiting Johannesburg, I boarded a plane for the three-hour flight to Cape Town. Shortly after takeoff, while reading some of the material I had bought at the museum, I noticed the guy next to me looking over my shoulder. He was a stocky, youthful forty-something, built like he could have played rugby back in the day.

Abruptly, he asked me a question:

"Do you think I'm evil?"

So what was I supposed to respond? Uh . . . nice country you got here. How 'bout them Springboks!

No. I was a captive audience.

I told him—Bernard's his name—that I didn't think he's evil. I thought that apartheid was evil and I was trying to understand it. I said that as an American I had nothing to crow about—in fact, we had Jim Crow at the same time he had apartheid, and we had slavery, to boot. America has given the world lots of bad things, from the KKK to Watergate to Rick Perry's hunting ranch.

I looked over but knew that would not make him feel better, because he was struggling with his past and I was not struggling with mine—though perhaps I should have been. I grew up in the Boston of the '70s busing crisis, and I was part of a Jewish community that had fled its inner-city roots and shed its civil-rights partnerships. The Boston of my youth was not all that different from the Jackson, Mississippi, depicted in the bestseller and hit film *The Help*. And that America was not all that different from the South Africa of Bernard's youth. In all these places, racism infected all strata of society, from City Hall to the Ladies Auxiliary. It trickled from top to bottom, getting into the cracks and nooks and tough to get at places, where we might tell "the help" to give it another shot of Windex.

The disease of discrimination spreads from one generation to the next until everyone buys into its toxic lies, even the victims. It plays itself out at the lunch tables of Woolworth's and in the bathrooms and water fountains or wherever someone displays a Confederate flag or tells an ethnic joke. Enough people stood up to the hatred to relegate Jim Crow and apartheid to history's dung heap. Boston is now a diverse, inclusive city. But the disease remains.

I came to understand that apartheid was little more than a virulent combination of the same toxic brew that still threatens us today: religious extremism and fear. In 1948, right-wing Afrikaner leaders played to the suspicions of rising Communism and blended that with a belief that white domination is God's will.

In Jackson and Johannesburg, buses were segregated by race. In some parts of Israel, they are segregated by gender, as are banks, elevators, grocery stores, pizza parlors, and a corner snack shop in Jerusalem's Bukharian Quarter, which has a side entrance with a sign marked "Women Only."

Apartheid began with segregation. Any segregation, including excessive gender segregation, leads us down a slippery slope toward discrimination. I'm not necessarily calling for unisex bathrooms in ultra-Orthodox neighborhoods, but there is no religious basis for pizza with a *mechitza* (a partition segregating women in Orthodox synagogues) and the constant harassment of females. Yes, it's worse in Saudi Arabia and Iran. And yes, Israel's human rights record is commendable, considering the fact that not long ago those currently segregated buses were being blown up.

Before my trip this summer, I had no idea just how intensely Nelson Mandela is loved, both by his own countrymen (including the Jews) and around the world. When you read his words of reconciliation and visit his tiny cell on Robben Island, you grasp how easily he could have succumbed to the hatred and the fear. He could have crushed his oppressors and driven them into exile; instead, he embraced them, saying, "For to be free is not merely to cast off one's chains, but to live in a way that respects and enhances the freedom of others."

When I posted on Facebook how Mandela is so loved, a rabbinic colleague replied, "Too bad he is anti-Israel."

Not true. Mandela has stated, "I cannot conceive of Israel with-drawing if Arab states do not recognize Israel, within secure borders."

Think about how counterproductive it is to label as anti-Israel a person who has lived his entire life promoting human rights. That puts Israel on the wrong side of history.

I'm not sure what the right side of history is, but I know that Mandela is on it. The Jewish people have always been there, too, as vanguards of justice and compassion. We invented the right side of history at the Red Sea and Sinai. The right side of history loves the stranger; it's eight lanes apart from playing the victim and has no exit marked "fear." It does not allow discrimination, hatred, and religious extremism to rule. Johannesburg and Jackson have been struggling mightily to board the bus headed that way.

I pray that Israelis might board it, too . . . and sit wherever they want.

Mensch•Mark 37

2015

PIERCING THE HEAVENS

The Purest Form of Prayer

Caring for those with special needs has always been one of my highest priorities, a crusade championed by my father, who fought to make sure that my brother, Mark, would always have a home in his community. Before my dad founded Humanity House in Brookline, people like Mark often ended up in institutions. Mark could never have had a Bar Mitzvah, but he did love to say the blessings on Friday night. Seeing him hold up the wine cup and sing along with the Kiddush is one of my most indelible childhood memories, one that came back to me while watching a Bar Mitzvah student's spirit soar.

We learn in the Talmud, "There is no person who does not have his hour." On a Shabbat morning very soon, a remarkable young man will ascend to the Torah to become Bar Mitzvah in my synagogue, on the very same pulpit where his bris took place thirteen years prior. His name is Jewels Harrison.

Because of his degree of autism, Jewels's capacity for speech is very limited, but he has found innovative ways to sing God's praises. In only a short amount of time, Jewels has become an accomplished pianist. He doesn't read music but is able to hear and reproduce it in detail. Innovative rows of pictures and symbols helped him identify and associate songs to play.

For his mitzvah project, Jewels has been performing at small parlor recitals, raising money for programs that will benefit other kids with special needs. His playing is extraordinary for any child his age, but especially for one who has spent so much of his life with a severely limited ability to communicate.

To hear Jewels play is to hear the shepherd boy's flute in the iconic Hasidic tale of the Baal Shem Tov. Moved by his first exposure to the powerful Yom Kippur service, though unable to read or understand the liturgy, that boy prayed in the manner he knew best. The congregation was aghast and looked to evict the boy, until the rabbi indicated from the pulpit that those shrill sounds of the whistle were able to pierce the heavens so that the prayers of the entire congregation might ascend.

Jewels is also preparing to lead many of the prayers of the service with his voice. Through arduous work and much patience, he will do just fine, but for the hundreds who will be attending, perfection will not be pertinent. What will matter is that we bear witness to Jewels's resounding statement that every human being has his hour, every life has infinite value, and everyone is equal in the eyes of God.

In their book *Practical Medical Halacha*, Fred Rosner and Moses Tendler state that Jewish law urges those with special needs "to achieve their fullest potential as Jews, while exhorting society to assist them in making their religious observance possible." In the Talmud, after all (Eruvin 54b), Rabbi Preida had a student with a severe learning disability, to the point where he needed to repeat each lesson four hundred times before the student understood it. Such patience needs to be applied across the board, and to a degree, that is happening.

Israel's Conservative Movement (Masorti) has been running a Bar Mitzvah program for special needs kids in Rehovot that has been attacked by Orthodox rabbis for many years. Just as Conservative Judaism has incorporated relevant contemporary data to reassess longstanding views regarding feminism and homosexuality, so did it long ago find ways to incorporate into ritual practice contemporary understandings of mental impairment and genetic disorders. As with women and LGBTQ, the purpose of implementing changes to long-held practices is to affirm the dignity of these individuals. As Jewish sources repeat time after time, the dignity of the individual should always be paramount.

I've led many memorable Bar and Bat Mitzvahs of children with special needs. One of my first was for Mitchell Levitz, a young man with Down syndrome, who used the Bar Mitzvah process as a springboard to living an exemplary life in leadership and advocacy. Today, three decades later, he is often in Washington articulating his cause and lobbying for better legislation. He's cowritten a book (which became a TV movie) detailing his experiences. Had Mitchell grown up in Rehovot, God only knows if he would have had such opportunities or gained such confidence. It would have been the world's loss.

When I was twelve, I got into the only fistfight of my life. It was when a kid started mocking my brother because of his special needs, laughingly calling him a "retard." Nowadays few things bring out the moral outrage in me as much as the abuse of innocent young children with disabilities.

Children with such challenges have so much to offer and often can't stand up for themselves when mistreated. Many can't speak at all. Oftentimes they are too trusting of those who take advantage of them.

Few things validate my decision to become a rabbi and represent the eternal message of Sinai more than seeing children like Jewels ascend to the Torah and pierce the heavens with a prayer so intense and pure that it just might save us all.

Mensch•Mark 38

MARCHING FOR OUR LIVES, RIDING ON SHABBAT

Sometimes Fulfilling God's Command Can Only Be Done by Violating It

I'll be joining local teens on the March for Our Lives on Saturday, and by traveling I will violate the Jewish Sabbath to get there. But in doing so, I'll fulfill the greatest of Jewish religious duties, one that supersedes even the Sabbath itself.

Yes, this march is so important that I—a rabbi—am going to blatantly disrupt God's holy Sabbath. But if the ancient rabbinic sages are to be believed, that's precisely what God wants me to do.

The obligation to save lives overrules virtually all other Jewish laws, and this march, if successful, will surely save lives. I can think of no better way to dramatize both the historic magnitude and the religious significance of this march than to hop on the "Shab-bus."

Countless lives are hanging in the balance right now. If this massive nationwide demonstration leads to real change, who knows how many lives will be spared the next time a deranged individual is denied an AR-15 because of strengthened, commonsense gun laws.

The last time I marched with the masses for stricter gun laws, in downtown Hartford two months after Sandy Hook, the result was dramatic. Realizing that the National Rifle Association's political clout was now being vigorously challenged by the popular will, the Connecticut state government proceeded to ban more than 150 assault-style gun models, along with magazines having a capacity greater than ten rounds. The state also implemented a universal background check system and required a permit to buy guns and ammunition. As a result, gun homicides in my home state were cut in half.

That rally did not take place on Shabbat, so it was a no-brainer for me to go.

This one is different.

The religious obligation in question is called *Pikuach Nefesh* in Hebrew and is derived from Leviticus 18:5, which states, "You shall keep My laws and rules, by the pursuit of which people shall live; I am the Lord." Other biblical verses reinforce the message that laws are intended to sanctify and preserve life, not to cause undue risk of death.

Judaism has always promoted a culture of life (it bears noting that in Jewish sources, human life is defined as beginning at or about the time of birth). The Talmud states that to save a single life is equivalent to saving the world. The children at Sandy Hook and the teens in Parkland, along with the slain of Las Vegas, Sutherland Springs, Orlando, and so many other places, add up to tens of thousands of victims of gun violence per year—tens of thousands of worlds destroyed. These unbearable and intolerable losses have fueled my decision to become a one-time conscientious objector toward Sabbath rest. If so many victims are not resting in peace, how can I allow myself to rest at all?

Pikuach Nefesh can be applied in many situations, but most often it is discussed regarding Shabbat. In the second century BCE, Seleucid armies adopted the strategy of attacking Jewish renegades on Shabbat. The Jews offered little resistance and were slaughtered. In 1 Maccabees, the Hasmonean patriarch Mattathias rejected that blind piety, stating, "If anyone comes against us on the Sabbath day, we shall fight against him and not all die as our brothers did in their hiding places."

The Talmudic sages taught that one who is vigilant in saving a life on Shabbat is praiseworthy. The Talmud presents several scenarios involving permissible Sabbath violations, including rescuing a child from a pit or saving someone drowning in the sea. The rabbis applied the principles of Pikuach Nefesh to saving the lives of both Jews and gentiles and made it clear that the risk of death did not need to be certain or immediate.

The most famous case in modern times—and the one most analogous to the march—occurred during a cholera epidemic in 1848, when Rabbi Israel Salanter stood before his community on Yom Kippur and encouraged them to end their fast prematurely. He dramatized that plea by eating and drinking in front of them.

In an account written eight decades later, Salanter is said to have stated, "There are times when one must turn aside from the Law, if by doing so a whole community may be saved. With the consent of the All-Present and with the consent of this congregation, we give leave to eat and drink on the Day of Atonement."

Salanter's advice did not directly save any lives, and, in fact, contemporary opponents noted that many thousands of Jews in those same lands who disregarded his gesture survived. But it is conceivable that some who were in a weakened state would have become sick had they not cut short their fasts. The mere chance that his life-affirming act could have limited the spread of that deadly disease was sufficient to warrant his gesture.

My boarding that bus or riding in that car will likely not save any lives directly. But by linking the voices of Parkland to the Voice of Sinai, I can elevate the conversation on guns in our country, helping legislators and voters—and the teens themselves—to appreciate the urgency of now. Meanwhile, I'll refrain from spending money or using my phone, and I'll chant a psalm or two, and my rolling Sabbath may become, for me and the teens I join, the most meaningful Sabbath we've ever experienced.

At Selma, Rabbi Abraham Joshua Heschel, who marched alongside Martin Luther King Jr., remarked that he felt like he was praying with his feet. On March 24, I will be praying with my feet, too. And while I walk, I'll be praying that, in some small way, I'll be saving lives, and thereby, just maybe, helping to save the world.

Mensch•Mark 39

1996

GOING, GOING, GONE

*Overcoming Tribal Loyalties for
the Voice of the Yankees*

I've had the privilege to count among my congregants numerous doctors, judges, lawyers, entertainers, journalists, politicians, and a US Senator. Since my goal as a pastor has always been to create an environment in which we can take off masks and be fully human, I've always been impressed at how eager celebrities are to do just that. No one more so than the great voice of the Yankees, Mel Allen. On a rainy June 19, 1996, Mel's funeral took place in my sanctuary. About seven hundred attended, including people from all walks of life and a Hall of Fame "who's who" of former players, baseball officials, and journalists. Joe DiMaggio sat in the second row near Whitey Ford and Joe Pepitone. George Steinbrenner sat on the aisle. Yogi Berra sat way in the back—he was still not on speaking terms with the club—next to Phil Rizzuto, Mike Lupica, and Bob Costas.

Mel, who never married, was closest to his sister, Esther Kaufman, who watched over him and safeguarded his legacy. She was very concerned that the eulogy given for Mel be absolutely on point. And she entrusted me, a lifelong fan of the enemy Boston Red Sox, with that job.

So I stood up behind my pulpit, staring down at the immortals, knowing that in a real way I was eulogizing not only a man but an entire bygone era. The Yankee dynasty was about to be reborn, but baseball had lost its innocence forever.

A prayer Jews recite three times daily is known as the *Amida*. This is in many ways our most significant prayer, containing within it the essence of our personal and collective aspirations. And it begins with a peculiar line, always recited silently, taken from Psalm 51:

"*Lord*, open my lips that my words might speak your praise."

This phrase is actually a prayer that we be able to pray, for Judaism is a faith that emphasizes the significance of each word and considers each word uttered with perfect authenticity a prayer. Each breath is a prayer, each utterance, if authentic, is an expression of our godliness. Each sentence, if it comes from the soul, is testimony to the wonder of being alive, of the miracles that God has given us.

Mel Allen's life was one long, extended, exhaustive, exhilarating, triumphant prayer. It was a call to all of us to see the sublimity in the smallest things, the pitch one inch off the corner, the stolen sign, the first seasonal shifts of the wind. And as for the larger things, he coined the most sublime expression of wonder of all, radical amazement in three short words: "How about that!" To have lived to be able to witness something worth a "How about that!" to him was a gift. Whether it was a triple play or a mammoth clout, with those three words, Mel Allen was able to elevate broadcasting to the realm of prayer, not just for him, but for the millions who clung to every word he spoke. And he was so fortunate, and he knew it, to have seen Gehrig and Ruth, to have chronicled the heroic deeds of Mantle and DiMaggio, to have placed the imprint of the bard on Don Larson's moment, to have helped us all to say week after week, night after night, "How about that!"

Mel Allen was a good, humble, and sensitive man. He was a loving son who took care of his parents in their old age. Through his sensitivity, he led his parents to believe that they were moving up here from Alabama to help him. When his father was ill, he said to them, "I need you to make a home for me up here." Such exquisite sensitivity. And after they passed on, they continued to be in his thoughts. Every year at our memorial service in the cemetery next door, Mel would be there with his sister, Esther, of course, to remember.

Imagine the kindness of this man, a man in a position to be overpowering and cruel and get away with it, but not Mel. He understood the sheer miracle of his good fortune in life and recognized the power of his words. Imagine, his was a voice that spoke many millions of words, so many millions, heard by many millions of people. Yet how few of those words were spoken in anger or bitterness, how few shaming another person, how few containing the gossip that poisons today's vernacular, and how many simple words of wonder and praise. It was as if every time he sat in front of a microphone or otherwise opened his mouth, he uttered that line from psalms, "Lord, open my lips so that my words might speak your praise."

Mel would probably be laughing right now because of his humility, and he never spoke of death, never really prepared himself or us for this moment. He wouldn't have wanted us to make a big deal: we're talking about a man who in grammar school was allowed to skip a grade in the middle of the year and he never thought to tell his parents. But with all due respect to his humility, we must speak his praise. Bert Parks once called him the nicest man in the whole industry. Walter Cronkite telephoned him at home a short while back, which really touched Mel. While the two had been at the same network, they hardly ever conversed, but Walter wanted to thank him, decades after the fact, for being so kind in showing him around the studio when he was just starting out.

In the '50s when Mel was at the height of his career, he received a call from an assistant football coach in the Midwest who had some interest in being a sportscaster. Mel Allen spent over an hour with this young man on the phone and left a lasting impression. It was only years later that George Steinbrenner reminded him of the incident.

His kindness went beyond normal expectations. As a teacher in Alabama, he once gave a failing grade to Bear Bryant. But he did it nicely. And in his twenties, Mel Allen actually decked someone, a Klansman. He beat the tar out of him, and then years later he found out that the guy was living in Connecticut, so Mel called him and said, "You want another lickin'?" The man couldn't remember who it was, so Mel took him to lunch. It says in Proverbs, "If your enemy be hungry, give him bread to eat." Mel had a knack for turning enemies into friends.

When we think of Mel Allen, it will be with that microphone in front of him, but let us first recall the kind words that always came out of the mouth that spoke into that mike. He achieved greatness through hard work, good fortune, and genuine talent but never through malice, deceit, or backstabbing. He achieved every honor imaginable. He is a resident of several Halls of Fame, but it didn't change him one bit.

And when we think of Mel, inevitably we think of baseball. Undoubtedly, some of you are here today mourning not only the loss of a good person but the end of an era, a time when baseball reminded us of all that was good, an innocence that baseball has long since lost but Mel himself maintained until the end. We felt that as long as Mel was with us, maybe we could regain that lost youth, that passion, that innocence.

But here we are: today is the day when the man who coined the name Joltin' Joe has left and gone away. Baseball's era of gentility lies before us.

And we are here to mourn the silencing of that voice. A journalist once called him the Homer of homers. Now that can be taken in many ways, but the intention was to designate Mel as the Homeric poet of the home run. His magnificent descriptive talents were on display especially when the drama hit its heights, and this gift was matched perfectly with a team and a time that immortalized him as he immortalized them. Another journalist once exclaimed that his voice had been decorated by a florist. I can see that. It resonated with class, style, and a combination of Southern grace and Jewish irony. His fabulous sense of humor, well that was both Southern and Jewish. Night after night, October after October, Mel Allen composed the epic poem of baseball's Homeric age. And for that he'll live on long after most of the heroes he described have faded from memory.

Most who knew Mel know that his passion for his work was unquenchable. He never really stopped working. Just over the past several days, he was making preparations to return to *This Week in Baseball*. Through an illness that would have stopped lesser men, I saw Mel struggling, and at times doubting it all, but never willing to give in to it. For him, giving up his work and his game would have meant giving in. He didn't keep working for ego or status. Undoubtedly, it gave him satisfaction to be appreciated, for I know how much it meant to him to be so much a part of the Yankee family. But Mel didn't do this for the glory. To silence his voice would have been to silence his soul.

Two years ago, just hours prior to Yom Kippur, baseball officially canceled the World Series for the first time in Mel's lifetime. People everywhere were in deep mourning. How could it be fall without the Fall Classic? Where would our heroes come from? What would become of our nation without our national pastime? The baseball world, the country, and the calendar were entering an autumnal abyss.

I wasn't sure what to say to Mel that evening. I wanted to comfort him in the hope that he could comfort me. So I said to him, "Such a sad day." And Mel, in his matter of fact way, which could often mask deep wisdom as plain common sense, replied, "This is not a tragedy. War, now that's tragic. Poverty and hunger, that's a tragedy. This is not a tragedy."

And I ascended this pulpit that night a whole lot wiser. Mr. Baseball, the one I had thought lived and breathed only for the game, made me understand that it was just a game, which lived and breathed through him but only inasmuch as it expressed the drama, beauty, and poetry of life. It wasn't the game that mattered; it was the living and breathing. It was on that night that the voice of the Yankees enabled this Red Sox fan to understand that, ultimately, we are all on the same team.

Mr. Baseball had his priorities straight. So while he will best be remembered for his association with the sport, and while one of his final activities was watching the Yankees win on Sunday, let us never forget the lesson he taught me that night. Let us mourn today not because baseball has severed its final tie to innocence but because the human race has lost a voice that brought us closer to one another and closer to God. And let us celebrate today, too. For Mel's voice, which was his essence, which became the essence of his sport, will never be silenced. The Lord opened his mouth, his words spoke God's praise, and those words will reverberate unto eternity.

May that voice continue to resonate through the heavens and through our souls, and may his gentle spirit be bound up in the web of life.

Mensch•Mark 40

2018

SHOULD JEWS TURN THE OTHER CHEEK?

Looking Evil in the Eye

The attack on Jewish worshipers in Pittsburgh in October 2018 hit me very personally. My mother's funeral was the same weekend, so for me and my community, it was truly a tale of two shivas. I sat publicly for ten hours each day because I believe in the importance of that ritual and in its healing power, and those endless hours enabled me to have real conversations with about 400 people. While people came to comfort me, they also looked to me for comfort, and our collective Jewish people's shiva and my personal shiva fused together as one. We sat together and mourned the untimely deaths of innocent, vulnerable people; people at prayer, people who had only love in their hearts. I felt helpless to do anything about it— and yet, in my community, the healing took place, down in the trenches of the mourning bench, one on one on one on one. The following essay arose from one of the many profound questions that percolated that week.

In the wake of the Tree of Life attack in Pittsburgh, among the unresolved issues is one that may not seem very significant when compared to the stinging loss of eleven innocent lives, but is vexing nonetheless: should Jews turn the other cheek?

A few days after the attack, the Rev. Eric S. C. Manning, leader of the Emanuel African Methodist Episcopal Church in Charleston, South Carolina, where nine parishioners were murdered in 2015, paid a shiva call to Pittsburgh, where he embraced Rabbi Jeffrey Myers of the Tree of Life congregation. Their shared grief moved us all, but at the same time it brought attention to one aspect of the two cases that wasn't shared.

Following the Charleston attack, the victims' families famously forgave the murderer as he stood before them in court. By contrast, as *The New York Times* reported, the Jews of Pittsburgh had no intentions of being so forgiving. The *Times* article states that Jews interviewed said they had been too busy burying the dead and trekking from shiva to shiva to devote much thought to the killer. It then adds, "But Jewish theologians also explained that their tradition, rooted more in the retributive justice of the Old Testament than the turn-the-cheek ethos of the New Testament, takes a different approach to forgiveness."

Yes, it's true, Judaism does take a different approach. The article goes on to explain, correctly, that the Jewish concept of *teshuvah* calls on the perpetrator to seek forgiveness from the victim before having any hope of absolution. Then it adds that Pittsburgh mourners "felt little instinct to forgive the person responsible for such horror."

Clearly, there is a difference in how the victims of Pittsburgh and Charleston approached similar calamities. But whenever someone traces things back to the "retributive justice of the Old Testament God," an enormous red flag is raised. There are many images of God depicted in the Hebrew Bible, some more vengeful and others more loving. The thunderous God of the Exodus Sinai narrative is later encountered by

Elijah, in the very same place, as a "still, small voice." And that kinder, gentler New Testament God seemed to conveniently forget to turn-the-cheek during the Crusades and Inquisition.

The notion of a perpetually vengeful Old Testament God has inspired stereotypic images of hard-hearted Jews, even though the Torah explicitly prohibits taking revenge and holding grudges.

Why does Judaism not encourage the unconditional embrace of your enemy? When you turn your cheek, you are no longer looking at your offender in the eye, face-to-face. True reconciliation can only occur when two human beings can truly see what is human in the other, and how each of us is created in the Divine image. But there are times when such authentic encounters simply can't happen. The Pittsburgh perpetrator showed no signs of remorse during his appearance in court, and it is doubtful that he will when he stands trial. It would be a grave injustice to blindly forgive him.

After the Charleston massacre, I attended a prayer vigil, at which I heard a presentation by Inni Kaur, a representative of the Stamford Sikh community, reflecting on her own faith group's experiences.

It should be noted that the Sikh community suffered a similar massacre, at a temple in Oak Creek, Wisconsin, in 2012. Unfortunately, no religious group is immune to such attacks. The image of people at prayer or study seeing their sanctuary violated, having the pastoral serenity and love of neighbor rendered instantaneously into a garish nightmare, is one that cuts across cultures.

My Sikh friend recalled Oak Creek, and how the community rallied together and preached love over hate, and, like Charleston, even forgave the perpetrator. She said, "These communities have shown us that faith helps endure any hardship, even the most unspeakable suffering. Faith does not mean we forget pain or grief. Faith means that we live free of hate. These monumental acts of forgiveness compel each and every one of us to work towards ending the racial terror that exists in our country today; to find ways to look beyond the boundaries of race, color, ethnicity and see the Oneness in all."

So "forgiving" enemies are not about letting them off the hook—it's about looking them in the eye and telling them, loud and clear, that they have not succeeded in driving a wedge between groups. It's about achieving a greater societal goal by suppressing base urges. In Charleston, Oak Creek, Orlando, and now Pittsburgh, the ideology of hate was drowned in a sea of love.

In Charleston, the victims' supreme gesture of love yielded tangible results—the removal of the Confederate flag from the state capitol. One hate-driven young man accomplished in one evening what Martin Luther King could not accomplish in a lifetime, at least with regard to the shunning of this symbol of hate.

One might say that for the bereaved of Charleston, forgiveness was the best revenge.

For the Jews of Pittsburgh, the best revenge against the particular hatred espoused by white nationalists has not been to turn the other cheek, but to build stronger bridges to other targeted communities, like African Americans and Muslims, who have shown such love in the wake of the attack.

And that love was reflected at the ballot box, where polls suggest that late deciders in the 2018 midterm elections swung away from harsh nativism, following pipe bomb attacks on Democratic leaders and the Pittsburgh pogrom. (Yes, these days pogroms no longer require angry mobs with pitchforks; now all it takes is a single crazy hater with an AR-15.)

As voters decided "enough is enough," our newest Jewish martyrs changed America, while the bereaved turned not the other cheek, but perhaps the tide of history.

Mensch•Mark 41

2007

GETTING FROM "I" TO "WII"

Overcoming Selfishness as a Key to Happiness

Nikos Kazantzakis wrote in his autobiography, "Reach what you cannot," a philosophy of striving that has inspired me throughout my life (see Mensch•Mark 26, "The Towers"). But poet Mary Oliver counters with this: "There are things you can't reach. But you can reach out to them, and all day long." Even when we've tired of reaching, we should never stop reaching out. This is adapted from a High Holidays sermon.

Human beings need to take their cues from other species. In the summer of 2007, just after Mara and I had sent Ethan and Dan off to camp, we went to Cape Cod, where for several days people were pre-occupied by the spectacle of fifty-five pilot whales that had beached themselves off Dennis. Forty-six were saved and sent back to sea, only to come ashore again the next day in Eastham, twenty-five miles north. The experts were at a loss as to why this could have happened. Writing in *The New York Times*, oceanographic scientist Peter Tyack explained that part of the reason was that family ties are very strong for pilot whales. They stay together no matter what, several generations of them, and if some are sick and end up leading the rest toward the beach, the healthy ones will follow. And when the forty-six healthy ones were escorted out to sea in Dennis, they came back to shore looking for the eleven who had died. As Tyack put it, "Mass strandings thus seem to be a tragic consequence of social bonding—which is particularly intense in pilot whales."

Think about your own family. Let's say we're all pilot whales. Would you have headed back to Dennis for the sake of that whale sitting next to you, or would you have gone out to sea? Whales are intelligent animals. I've got to think that somewhere in their little brains they understood that there was no way to save those eleven loved ones and that they were just committing mass blubbercide by turning around. But they couldn't imagine going on living without the stranded eleven, and the family could not survive the drastic transformation of Cape Cod Bay at low tide. So there were the whales, exemplars of family stick-togetherness; here I was, Mr. Advanced Species, sending my kids out into the mosquito-infested wilds of New England, into the hands of total strangers for weeks of incessant bathroom humor, institutional food, searing heat, and wedgies. We have a lot to learn from the whales.

So I'm at the International House of Pancakes a couple of months earlier, up near Boston, in Watertown. I'm sitting at a table near the register, having breakfast with my brother, Mark (see Mensch•Mark 14, "My Brother's Keeper"). Belgian waffles for me, and he's having scrambled eggs and a Diet Coke, which he downs right away.

My mind is wandering. I look at the IHOP logo and shake my head at the amazing good fortune of this chain, that they had the prefix "I" long before it became cool. Long before iTunes and iPods and iBooks and iHome and iVillage and iSafe and iParty and iThis and iThat, and the just-released iPhone, there was IHOP. Suddenly IHOP, the most uncool place on earth this side of Howard Johnson, is reaping the benefits of its first letter.

We've gone from the "me" generation of the '70s to what now has become the "I" generation. One could easily make the claim that Rosh Hashanah and Yom Kippur have become, in fact, the "iHoly Days." We focus so much on our personal experience and what God has done for *me* lately. It's all about me!

I wondered, when will we begin the age of "we"? I was looking for a sign.

And then my lucky day arrived. It was mid-spring when my shipment came in. I stopped by the mall on a whim and the EBX store just happened to have gotten it in, literally, only minutes before my arrival. The case was not even open, but there it was: the Wii video game system that my kids had been begging for since Hanukkah.

Was this a sign, I wondered? Are we finally beginning to go from "I" to "Wii"?

I'm thinking about all these things and then the waitress at IHOP does something that takes my breath away. She returns to the table with a smile, bearing an unsolicited refill of Diet Coke for Mark. I didn't ask for it. She just brought it. Just like that. A new cup. Filled to the top.

Now, my brother will often attract sympathetic attention because of his clearly noticeable disabilities. But never, *never* before had anyone ever brought him a drink refill without first asking if he wanted it. Of course he wanted it, but that was beside the point. Do they always do this, I wondered, or was this waitress just being nice because of my brother? Something simply overwhelmed me at that moment, nearly bringing me to tears. I didn't know this waitress from Adam, but I sat there wondering what drove her to an act of such immaculate goodness.

I tried to imagine her life. Five mouths to feed back in Southie... Dad at the VA hospital in Chelsea... the IHOP gig is her first steady job in years... got up at 4 AM to beat the traffic to Watertown before her shift begins.

But what drove her to show that little bit of extra kindness for my brother? Does her brother have fragile X syndrome as well? Is it company policy? Was it for the tip? (Okay, I gave a nice tip.) Or was being nice simply a marketing tool adopted by IHOP in an age when we are all so desperate for a little human kindness, when all we want is for someone somewhere to take us from I to we?

Then that summer it happened again, this time at a pizza place in St. Louis, where we traveled with our kids on a college scouting trip. Free refills are not what I was looking for; they are a dime a dozen. Burger King now offers free refills. There's even a website, a national movement for free refills.

It's free *unsolicited* refills that I sought, like Rebecca in Genesis offering unsolicited water for Eliezer's camels.

I know that some people find waitstaff hovering over them annoying, and parents certainly have a right to regulate what is offered to their children. But it is precisely that act of spontaneous kindness that by its sheer simplicity can help to reverse the trend and get us from I to we.

I grew up in a more genteel age. I tell my kids that there was a time when at the gas station attendants used to check the oil and wash the windshield, when, in fact, *other people* used to fill the tank. In the newspaper they used to have a section called "Lost and Found." Now when something is lost, we just assume it's never coming back. People used to look after one another. Now, no one even looks *at* other people. Perhaps we would if eye contact were spelled *iContact*.

I took Dan (then fourteen) to Madame Tussauds wax museum in Times Square and performed an experiment by lining myself up to look directly into the eyes of some of the wax figures. I looked for someone my height, which left me with Napoleon and Shakira. It was uncanny. It was like they were looking directly at me and yet right through me. There is something about eye contact that goes beyond the physiological. Two souls touching.

Though not so much with wax.

A few weeks later I was back in Midtown Manhattan and tried it out on some real people. I looked into the eyes of everyone coming at me, just to see if souls could touch. And amazingly, every set of eyes looked right through me, just like Napoleon's had. They were looking at me... but not. It reminded me of how dehumanizing the city can be. I looked for any sign of acknowledgment. Finally, I ducked into a Judaica store, and even there no one greeted me. No one looked at me. And I was wearing a yarmulke! At Virgin Records someone asked me for the time. But that doesn't count. Back out in the street, eye after eye, no one said hello; no one even smiled.

Finally, I saw someone coming at me, seeming to acknowledge, in some small way, that I exist.

"Sir," she said.

Yes, she was going to speak!

"Sir. You dropped your umbrella."

Indeed, I had. It had fallen from my backpack. I smiled, thanked her, and went on.

Eye contact is not merely an act of recognition; it is an act of giving. It is the sharing of one's humanness. In the animal kingdom it may be seen as a threat; in some Asian and Middle Eastern societies it's impolite. But people the world over have rituals expressing a desire for simple human connection. It reorients us; it gets us from I to we.

In Africa, the ritual of a handshake is far more elaborate than anything we do. One Peace Corps blogger counted up to twenty-eight mini handshakes in one encounter he witnessed in Gambia. And with hands holding the other person's wrist, the response to each of a series of questions is always, "In peace."

"Peace be with you."

"Peace be with you."

"How is work?"

"In peace."

"How is the family?"

"In peace."

"How is the wife?"

"In peace."

"How is your brother?"

"In peace."

It's interesting that Jews do something quite similar with the greeting Shalom, which means "peace." But it also gets in both "hello" and "good-bye," reminding us that every hello has a little good-bye in it and vice versa. It is a wonderfully nuanced greeting.

I just love visiting day in camp. You get three hours of "hello," followed by three hours of "good-bye." Somewhere in the middle is an hour of a perfectly balanced "Shalom."

It's really a paradigm for all of life. We spend the first half of it saying hello and the second half immersed in a long, endless good-bye. Until it ends with Shalom, which we say as the coffin is being lowered into the grave.

In any relationship, we never stop saying "Shalom," so that we never completely give up the excitement of that first hello, even when we are saying that final good-bye.

The Talmud says of Yochanan ben Zakkai, the greatest rabbi of his era, that "no one greeted him first, even the Gentile in the marketplace." He could have rested on his laurels and waited for people to come to him. He lived at a time when Jews were fighting Romans for survival—and, as always, Jews were fighting other Jews, too. But it didn't matter to him. Yochanan saw that every other human being is created in God's image, and he made it his business to greet them . . . and to do it *first*.

So maybe we've turned a corner, but the true test of that is what happens when we literally turn the corner, when we're walking on the street and seeing people. In his masterful book on Jewish ethics, Joseph Telushkin cites Rabbi Chaim Ozer Grodzensky, who told a young student who had moved to Vilna, "When I lived in a small town before I came to Vilna, I was very scrupulous to cheerfully greet every person I met on the street. But since I came to Vilna, I stopped this practice, because in the big city, it is impossible to greet everyone. Still it is appropriate to greet those whose eye we catch, and all of those whom we know, if only slightly."

Do we do this? Are we always smiling? On the subway? Do we look up? Do we acknowledge the basic humanity and godliness even of total strangers? New York is the ultimate test. If basic kindness can make it there, it can make it anywhere.

As a rabbi I have become especially attuned to how people try to read my body language. But this advice applies for everyone. People who are naturally shy or are feeling depressed may not realize that their scowl appears to others as standoffish and angry. We're not very good at reading faces, and we're even worse at reading faceless letters and emails. When you can't look into the eyes, you can't really see into the soul.

The medieval Talmudist Rabbi Menachem ha-Me'iri said that even when we resent a visitor's intrusion, we should *still* act as if we are happy to see him.

Rabbi Israel Salanter, the nineteenth century rabbi, saw a scholar with a forlorn look on his face during the days between Rosh Hashanah and Yom Kippur. The scholar said he was worried because these are the days when God is judging us. To which Salanter replied, "But other people won't realize that that's what's bothering you. They might think that you are upset with them."

Moodiness affects everyone around us. Parents take work worries out on their children or spouses. Children are often less sophisticated at reading our faces, especially if there are conflicts in the home or a divorce situation. Kids will often blame themselves, when that is the last thing the parent really wants. Jewish sources are telling us loud and clear that our moods do not really belong to us.

Even God understands this. Jewish law permits us to interrupt prayer in order to return a greeting. Why? Because that person who greeted you is also a manifestation of the divine image. Either way, we are still talking to God. We do not have the right to say to the world, "Mind your own business" because our business is their business, too, as we journey from I to we.

And somewhere along this journey, we can add a prayer for the doomed whales of Dennis and the waitress in Watertown.

Mensch•Mark 42

THE GOD OF LOVE

Inheriting a Family Legacy of Unconditional Love

To conclude this journey, I return to basic values that brought me to my calling in the first place: family, inclusiveness, and unconditional love. Reflecting on the God of love brings me back to the moment I decided to become a rabbi, during my senior year of college, just before my father died. For this final mensch•mark lesson, I am inspired by a startling encounter with my great-grandfather and a cousin who shares my Hebrew name. I am reminded of the true loving and inclusive nature of God and the call to a life of menschlichkeit.

I believe in a God of love.

Maybe one reason for this is that I was born on Valentine's Day. Or perhaps it has to do with a man who died many years before I was born. Or maybe both.

Once I was riding shotgun in a hearse on my way to a burial, criss-crossing Old Montefiore Cemetery in Queens and its densely packed, soaring monuments, a mini Manhattan for the dead. The hearse turned a corner and there, in the front row, staring me down, was my name—or more precisely, the person for whom I was named—chiseled into eternity. I had never seen my great-grandfather's grave before. Talk about your life flashing before your eyes. At that moment I felt a rush of recognition, as if a past life was flashing before mine.

I decided to learn more about him.

Joshua J. Kastan, a saintly and strictly observant Hasid, fell in love with a woman named Mollie. But family lore has it that when they were about to be married, Mollie refused to shave her head. One can only imagine the hubbub provoked by this breach of traditional practice. Yet Joshua was no fence-sitter. He stood by her and they were married, hair and all. He continued to love her through years of barrenness (attributed by detractors to her brazenness) and resisted the advice to leave her. Finally, miraculously, they had a daughter, my grandmother, Rebecca. To add one more romantic twist, Joshua and Mollie died on the same date, three years apart, August 19.

Rebecca, as fiery as her mother, married Samuel Hammerman, and they had seven children, one dying very young. Their home was filled with music and laughter. They scraped by on Samuel's income as a tailor. My uncle Saul described their home as being decorated in "wall to wall newspaper," but it was a home that was filled with love. To help earn money, my father, who had a lovely tenor voice, began to sing professionally. Eventually, he and his two brothers became cantors. Their fondest childhood memories included spending Shabbat afternoons together with all the cousins gathered in their Zeyde Joshua's home.

Rebecca and Sam had sixteen grandchildren, and fully a quarter of them were named for Joshua Kastan, including me, my cousins Jan and Jules, and my older cousin Jeffrey.

Jeff, an aspiring actor and poet, was serious, soft-spoken, and strikingly handsome. When I came to New York for rabbinical school in the late '70s, I got to know him quite well. Several years my senior, Jeff provided me a keyhole glimpse into some of the diversity of New York culture and, when he became HIV positive in the mid '80s, an insider's view of AIDS devastation as well. At about the same time that I moved to Stamford, coincidently so did Jeff with his partner, Seth. In late 1993, Jeff, who hadn't set foot in a synagogue since his Bar Mitzvah, shared his story from Beth El's pulpit. It was the kind of sermon our great-grandfather Joshua would have admired.

He said, "The God that I learned about in my home was a God of love, understanding, mercy, and reason. That God has given me real strength... His love for us is not measured by the absence of hardships. His love for us is the life he's given us."

He added: "To me the purpose of life is to learn, to grow. To do this, we choose problems to solve, or, more often, problems choose us. From the time we're born it is problems that stir us to grow. Well, I see HIV as one of these problems, a lesson, a test. It is not a test I would have chosen. But it's the test that life has brought me. My faith has held up to this test. I believe more than ever that there is a basic goodness to life and a reason for the things that happen."

Six years later, when I last saw Jeff in hospice, curled up in a fetal position and barely breathing, I understood that no God of mine could have afflicted him so mercilessly. Rather, I sensed the sanctity in every heroic gasp of air, in each moment of survival. I reached back for every ounce of *Hesed* (loving-kindness) I could summon and held his hand.

What I had grasped before intellectually now was imprinted on every fiber of my being: This is horrible. This is desperately unfair. But this is no divine punishment. This is not what God wants. What God wants is for us to love all the more.

At the very end, Jeffrey looked serene, content with having made every day count. He took a life sentence and made of it a life. A gardener, he grew petals around it. A brilliant writer, he added the exclamation point to his poem, his Torah, something we all need to do.

At his funeral, which took place in my window-encircled sanctuary, I read a poem Jeff had written decades earlier, when he was a teenager, called "Valentine to Man."

> *I listened to the music—*
> *And it sounded so sweet that I shouted up to heaven:*
> *"Let me love."*
> *And God spoke to me and He said . . .*
> *"You do love.*
> *You feel the sun rise and exalt as it travels*
> *Its long journey over its old road.*
> *You see the great green wonder rolling in and out,*
> *taking life from its depths of*
> *turbulence to its shores of peace.*
> *You hear the music of nature singing to you*
> *Ringing sweetly in your ears.*
> *You laugh and you cry, small yet large*
> *against the majesty of life.*
> *And while there is no one, nothing—*
> *You do love . . .*
> *And you breathe and sing along with the awkward,*
> *Beautiful melody . . .*
> *AND YOU KNOW ME,*
> *And you love."*

I reflected on all these life lessons at the very time my movement was grappling with whether to recognize LGBTQ rabbis. In Jeff's honor, I was fully in support.

Some come out of the closet. I came off the fence.

Either one is a leap of faith, an act of great courage. It is also an act of return, or *teshuvah*, for it is a return to your true values, to your deepest held beliefs, to who you were all along. And that leap of faith can only be made into the arms of a God of love.

Just after Passover in 2007, I brought my son Dan, then in eighth grade, to Old Montefiore Cemetery for a family history project, and when we looked closely at his great-great-grandfather Joshua's stone, I noticed something I'd never seen before, something that shook me to the core.

The Hebrew date of my great-grandfather's passing was the fifteenth of the month of Av, also known as Tu B'Av, the Jewish Valentine's Day, which occurs in the summer.

I was born on Valentine's Day, the one that occurs in February.

That Joshua's *yahrzeit* (anniversary of his death), in the strangest way, became *this* Joshua's birthday.

One generation dies, another is born, on the same day, one sanctified by the God of love. And so I wondered: As I try to forge a message that might outlast my precious tenure on earth, is it my voice that is speaking, or is it my great-grandfather's? Is the music my own, or is it my father's? Is my poetry my own, or is it Jeff's?

Somewhere in the mix of Joshua's piety, Molly's brazenness, the love and laughter that filled Rebecca's home, resides my father's call to me: to love, to give, and . . .

"Be a *mensch*."

Be a mensch.

The echo of that call carries me back to a day long before I saw my great-grandfather's grave at Old Montefiore. I'm carried back, past a thousand Bar Mitzvahs, past the mohel's knife, past Oreo cookies, the dove at the Kotel, past Crosby's Invisible Fence, and the kind waitress at IHOP. Way back, past Good Mrs. Murphy, past "A Young Rabbi."

Back to a blizzard, an envelope, and a decision.

* * *

The blizzard of the century was raging outside. It's February 7, 1978, a date when, thirteen years later, my first son would be born. But on this day, two and a half feet of snow fell outside my high-rise dorm in Providence. I looked outside my window and could see nothing but trees waving their branches at me like anxious cleanup hitters waiting for the pitch. The National Guard and the Army were called in. At least twelve were dead in Rhode Island alone. Massachusetts and Rhode Island both declared a state of emergency. No one was allowed on the streets. It wouldn't have mattered; the roads were impassible. Brown canceled classes for a week.

On day two of the storm, I woke up shivering, with a temperature of 102. I had nowhere to go and no way to get there. The term *progress* was rendered meaningless by this snow. Even Army jeeps were stuck in the drifts. The thick blanket of white wiped away history and smashed the idols of modernity. It was the biggest blizzard I ever have and likely ever will live through, the Blizzard of '78.

For three days it was just me in my small cubicle of a room on the corner of Thayer and Power, five floors up, overlooking a glistening Rhode Island snowscape (to be completely precise, once the snow stopped, my girlfriend, Mara, heroically trudged through the drifts to bring me the last carton of orange juice from Thayer Market). Just me and my droning TV with images of some or another governor sporting a sweater, speaking to us from some emergency shelter. Just me, the TV … and the letter.

The letter. The white letter. The one on my dresser. The one calling me to serve the Jewish people and God for the rest of my life.

I had gone to Brown to study Judaism, but there I fell in love with the vast range of religious expression and with the ways diverse cultures intersect. My favorite teacher taught Hinduism. I walked down the hill to the art museum at RISD to spend hours staring at the Dancing Shiva.

Ironically, it was the study of other faiths that led me back to Judaism. I returned via the back door, and now I was swerving my way toward the rabbinate and wasn't sure how to get my hydroplaning life under control in order to make this decision rationally. To this day, I don't understand what matter of thought led me to the rabbinate. But I know that it was not really a choice. It was, for lack of a better word, a calling.

"Go forth," the letter was crying to me Abrahamically at precisely the time when I was most unable to go *anywhere.* I was stuck in Providence, stuck in sickness, stuck in snow.

I later told the world that the rabbinate was selected by process of elimination. Law was too cutthroat, and medicine . . . well, part of being a vegetarian is that I can't stand the sight of blood. There was also journalism, my great passion, but I had soured on the idea of starting a career by covering fires in Podunk.

The last thing I ever expected to be was a rabbi. I had seen what being clergy had meant for my family: life in a fishbowl, scrutinized from birth, talked about in the aisles of Marshalls, blown Sunday outings sacrificed to someone else's funeral. I used to wait in the car as Dad popped over to plot seven for a quick unveiling, then it was off to Grandma's for some lunch. It's not a normal life.

But it's a beautiful life.

My mind wanders back to another snowy, wintry evening, when I was eleven or twelve. It was Hanukkah and my dad had procured two coveted tickets to a Boston Bruins game. Hockey was king in Boston back then and I had been anticipating this best-ever Hanukkah gift for weeks. We headed to the game but needed to make one stop on the way—at a V.A. hospital in Chelsea to light the holiday candles. With each traffic light slowing the already snail-like traffic near the Tobin Bridge,

I sensed that we might be late for the game. But once we reached the hospital, I was drawn like a moth to the dancing flames of those colorful candles, as reflected in the tearful eyes of the patients, many of whom were wheelchair bound. When we finally got to the Garden, the Zamboni was preparing the ice for the second period. But for me, it didn't matter that we were late. I felt so lucky to have shared that moment with my father. I can't for the life of me recall the final score of the game, but I'll never forget how, on an icy evening along the shores of the Mystic River, my dad's summons came through loud and clear.

"Be a mensch."

That might be the night when I was truly called to the rabbinate.

It's Friday in Providence, and the deadline is approaching. I need to respond. My fever is cooling and the snow has begun to melt. The letter stares at me from my dresser. I look at it again. It welcomes me for having chosen a "career dedicated to the study of our tradition and the service of our people." Do I really want that? What kind of life have I set out for myself? How can I, the prototypical outsider, find comfort among the suits? Rabbi: the epitome of the organization man . . . the instructor, the handshaking, small-talk-making, schmooze-slithery insider. Is *that* what I want to become? How can I fit in and yet retain a skeptical, outsider's perspective and change things? How will I find the time to be alone? How can I avoid losing my humanity in the process of becoming a role model? What does it even mean to be a role model? Does it imply that I have to playact a role?

Would my acceptance of a religious profession mark the end of my religious life?

Would I change the rabbinate, or would it change me?

As I lay in my bed, simmering and sweating—and really in need of a shower—I concluded that I would not lose that inner drive but just gain the means and language to express my convictions better and, as a bonus, an audience to hear them.

That hope grew powerful enough to raise me from my sickbed and propel me down the snowbanks of Thayer Street to the student union. And then, I lifted my arm to open the mailbox and dropped my acceptance form inside.

Something within whispered that this singular act will resonate long after the last bit of snow has melted, and that it would be for a blessing.

* * *

Now I'm reaching the other end of the book, the final chapters of a rabbinic career born in the icy streets of Chelsea and the drifts of Providence. I've gone from Genesis to Deuteronomy, and I'm looking up at the slopes of Nebo, knowing that my remaining time may be short.

Has it been well spent? I hear Tom Hanks, dying at the end of *Saving Private Ryan*, muttering, "Earn this," to the title character. Have I earned it? Have I fulfilled the Talmud's dictum, "In a place where there is no humanity, be human?" Have I been a worthy vessel for the kind of bottomless, unconditional love that my great-grandfather, father, and cousin bequeathed to me?

Less than a year after I mailed that acceptance letter, at a time when I was strongly considering leaving the seminary I had just entered, my father had the chutzpah to die, and that shock froze me in place. I was at the initial stages of a post-adolescent uprising against him, and he had to go and *die* on me, leaving me stuck with a rabbinical career as his final wish. Becoming a rabbi was now not so much a calling as a summons (and in my fouler moods, a sentencing), but no matter how I looked at it, the decision had never really been mine. But over the ensuing months and years, as my shock and paralysis melted away, my retreating anger gave way to my father's persistent summons—to be a *mensch*—and the growing recognition that *this* message was what I was put on this earth to share.

That's what I was called to be. Not a rabbi but a *mensch*. A human being of character.

A *human* rabbi.

The genius of the Talmud cries out to me:

In a world that lacks humanity, be human.

When Moses stood at the foot of Mount Nebo, he addressed the people in a rambling, haunting, bitter poem.

"Hey, listen up, you…give an ear! One ear! That's all I'm asking. Hey, you. Put away that phone! Stop with the texting!"

Moses must have stood there after that thoroughly demoralizing final sermon, chomping at the bit to hand over this stiff-necked, obstinate group to Joshua, his mind wandering back to those early days when he was but a child of eighty, and the fateful decisions he had made … the slain taskmaster, the burning bush …

"Why did I take off my goddam shoes at that farkakteh shrub? I should have just run the other way! Those kvetching people and their Gentleman's Agreement with their golden calves. Why am I here?"

And then I hear the voice again.

"*Be a* mensch*!*"

Enough, Dad! Enough. Enough. The fight is over. The Torah is written. The 613th commandment is in the books.

But the question remains:

Have I earned it?

Have I, in the end and throughout, through the forty-two steps of this passage, been and become a *mensch*?

If I have brought humanity and dignity to my work/worship/life—and that's not for me to answer—then I can trace it all back to that moment when I trudged through the snow to Faunce House during the Blizzard of '78, to place that rabbinical school acceptance letter in the mail slot. That was the turning point not only in my life but in the lives that, by some good fortune, I have had the opportunity to touch; all the people whose journeys have intersected with mine, the thousand Bar and Bat Mitzvahs, the kids at my first Tot Shabbat, the seniors I've visited and later buried. They were all with me when I put that envelope into the slot. And now, if you've gotten this far (without skipping too far ahead), you are, too.

I don't know if my work, my worship, has helped others to be more fully human. But I do know that it has helped me immensely. If I had not chosen this path, I would not be half the person I've become. And maybe, just maybe, my chosen path has helped you, too. I hope so.

One final lesson emerges from all this:

There are forty-two stops in the Wilderness journey, corresponding to forty-two stages of a person's growth, and there are thirty-two words in the Attributes of Divine Mercy, as laid out in Exodus 34:6–7:

> Lord, God, of mercy and kindness, long-suffering, and abundant in goodness and truth; keeping mercy unto the thousandth generation, forgiving iniquity and transgression and sin...

This passage is repeated often in Jewish liturgy, almost as a mantra, as a reminder to activate our most compassionate, most godly instincts. But the verses also include a phrase that the rabbis deliberately left out of the liturgical formulations:

> ...Who visits the iniquity of the parents upon the children, and upon the children's children, unto the third and unto the fourth generation.

Yet in the count of thirty-two words, this part needs to be left in; after all, our actions, whether positive or negative, *do* impact the lives of those who will come after us. My father's *menschlichkeit* was part of his legacy to me. Also, what might have been considered sinful by one generation might be understood differently by the next. The illicit, tenacious love of my great-grandparents for each other, which was widely condemned three generations ago, has become the foundation of my faith, my model for all that is kind, good, loving, godlike . . . and utterly human.

According to the Kabbalistic tool known as *Gematria,* whereby each Hebrew letter has a numerical equivalent, the value of the Hebrew word for heart (*lev*) is also thirty-two, and the value for the letter most often used to symbolize God (*yod*), is ten. So if you add God (10) to heart (32) you reach forty-two, the number of way stations on a human life-journey.

That equivalence yields a basic truth that has guided my life as it guided my great-grandparents' lives three generations ago. It has, in fact, been my guiding ethos since long before I came upon this earth, having been passed down through my veins through the generations, from Moses's disciple to Mollie's husband to Michal and Miriam's recently orphaned son—from *Joshua to Joshua to Joshua.*

That guiding ethos that is based on those thirty-two most *menschy* words from Sinai, those qualities of divine compassion, God's love poem to humanity, along with my forty-two step journey toward spiritual maturity, is this:

The God of Love has a human heart.

The formula is simple, yet it is the most profound life lesson for a human rabbi who believes in a God of love:

The God of Love has a human heart.

And so must I.